I just wrote this
five minutes ago...

Essays on contemporary poetry

Carl Watts

Edited by Shane Neilson
Cover and book design by Jeremy Luke Hill
Proofread by Carol Dilworth
Set in Linux Libertine
Printed on Mohawk Via Felt
Printed and bound by Arkay Design & Print

LIBRARY AND ARCHIVES CANADA CATALOGUING IN PUBLICATION

Title: I just wrote this five minutes ago… : essays on contemporary poetry / Carl
    Watts.
Names: Watts, Carl, 1983- author.
Identifiers: Canadiana (print) 20210372559 | Canadiana (ebook) 20210372575 |
    ISBN 9781774220542 (softcover) | ISBN 9781774220559 (PDF) |
    ISBN 9781774220580 (HTML)
Subjects: LCSH: Poetry. | LCSH: Poetry—Authorship. | LCSH: Poetry—History
    and criticism.
Classification: LCC PN1031 .W38 2022 | DDC 808.1—dc23

ONTARIO ARTS COUNCIL
CONSEIL DES ARTS DE L'ONTARIO
an Ontario government agency
un organisme du gouvernement de l'Ontario

Gordon Hill Press gratefully acknowledges the support of the Ontario Arts Council.

Gordon Hill Press respectfully acknowledges the ancestral homelands of the Attawandaron, Anishinaabe, Haudenosaunee, and Métis Peoples, and recognizes that we are situated on Treaty 3 territory, the traditional territory of Mississaugas of the Credit First Nation.

Gordon Hill Press also recognizes and supports the diverse persons who make up its community, regardless of race, age, culture, ability, ethnicity, nationality, gender identity and expression, sexual orientation, marital status, religious affiliation, and socioeconomic status.

Gordon Hill Press
130 Dublin Street North
Guelph, Ontario, Canada
N1H 4N4
www.gordonhillpress.com

Contents

Introduction   *v*

Part 1: WORKING POETRY CLASS

Make Work Mean   3

Reviewing Reviewing   21

I Just Wrote This Five Minutes Ago: 39

Minimal Requirements   47

Formatting Engagement   61

"Whatever she is, she is not nothing"   77

Part 2: EN GARDE

On Formalism   95

Whose Solitudes?   113

State of the Avant   123

Avant and the Future   135

What Were Lyrics?   145

Concluding Precariously   157

Bibliography   163

Introduction

"Before submitting, read one of our issues to get an idea of what kind of poems we publish". The ubiquity of the phrase will be apparent to anyone who has spent much time sending their poems to the seemingly limitless number of North American poetry journals. It speaks to the oddity of an art form that assumes those practicing it may not be quite as interested in consuming it, at least to the extent that they can recognize the distinctions between contemporary outlets and styles. It's a logical step from here to Frog Hollow Press' submissions site, which (as of May 2020) instructed prospective chapbook authors not to send a manuscript unless "you have been previously published in a trade book, chapbook or a recognized literary journal". A little earlier, in 2002, one finds the scholarly avant-garde lamenting that the little mainstream attention being paid to American poetry was based on similar ideas about the poet as everyman or generalist, like when Marjorie Perloff quips in an interview with Charles Bernstein that "*The New York Times* praised Dana Gioia precisely because he had worked for ten years for General Foods and made his mint before turning to poetry—evidently something one can do by a sheer act of will. One declares oneself a poet, period".

Do many people who have never seen a movie since *Gone with the Wind* think to record a film using their phone and then submit the results to a festival? No, but the differences between poetry and film are obvious in many ways—making movies requires more resources, technological skills, human capital, and time. Magazines that publish fiction also encourage potential contributors to have a look at what they're into; still, one gets the impression that poetry especially is a kind of writing for which prospective authors are in need of reminders that they should not only have written, but indeed just read a recent example of the form before submitting a poem of their own. Poetry is the only art in which it's standard for aspiring creators to assume they don't need any knowledge of the craft as it exists in the present.

Yet, in part for similar reasons, poetry is also comparatively free of fluke stories of immediate success, or the notion that a successful poet must have a mythically innate store of natural talent. Anyone might be able to do it, but getting there evidently takes some kind of work—even if that work produces something that would-be poetry practitioners themselves can't be trusted to recognize (hence magazines finding their slush piles so hopeless as to require pleas for people to pick up an issue before submitting). Absolutely anyone can recount a painful memory or turn a clever phrase on a cocktail napkin in language that's looser than formal prose and feel momentarily like they're a genius. But just about any stranger sitting next to them can read or listen to the words themselves and be sure that's not the case. A smaller number of strangers could tell our napkin-scribbler why that's not the case; a still more select group might deny it publication in *The New Yorker*. What I'm describing is less a hierarchy than a chain of knowing and not knowing that is as nebulous as it is somehow always intact. The point of this book is to explore the contours of the situation I've depicted with this deliberately half-baked image.

Another way of grappling with the dynamic I'm describing is to discuss the paradoxical uselessness of poetry. Let's re-theorize this approach, beginning with a short history: we'll start with W.H. Auden, who famously claimed that poetry "makes nothing happen". He did so in a poem—"In Memory of W.B. Yeats"—and, as Don Share and Angela Leighton have pointed out, respectively, the affirming valence of the original (preceding as it does the lines "it survives / In the valley of its making where executives / Would never want to tamper[...] / [...]it survives, / A way of happening, a mouth") is often obscured by those who conflate the soundbite with a similar line—about "the fallacious belief that art ever makes anything happen"—that itself comes from "The Public v. the Late Mr. William Butler Yeats", an elaborate essayistic set piece in which Yeats' mystical themes are debunked.[1]

Despite the foggy provenance of "poetry makes nothing happen", we find this attitude taken up pretty frequently. Charles Bernstein, for example, in "Provisional Institutions: Alternative Presses and Poetic Innovation", adapts a comment originally made by James Sherry in *L=A=N=G=U=A=G=E* that "a piece of paper with nothing on it has a definite economic value. If you print a poem on it, this value is lost". Avant-gardists of all stripes were combining Auden's and Bernstein's sentiments into chiasmatic pronouncements with such regularity that in 2018 you could find Christian Bök, in a piece called "Statements", packaging timeless poetry paradoxes and recent controversies into snappy formulations about the proliferation of poets ("Give a man a poem, and he will starve for a day, but teach a man to be a poet, and he will starve for a lifetime").[2] Indeed, the insistent chiasmus intones, the worthlessness of poetry stands as proof of the standing of poetry against worthlessness.

The futility dynamic's counterpart is the feel-good, which includes books like Stephanie Burt's *Close Calls with Nonsense: Reading New Poetry* (2009) and *The Poem Is You* (2016). Alongside their generative (and gentle) critical arguments, these volumes introduce many notable writers from the bewilderingly huge world of contemporary American poetry. Burt envisions the books as a collection of instructions and an introduction to US poetry written since 1980, respectively. While the second is geared towards readers who are unfamiliar with this universe as well as those "who know that space—or parts of it—well", the question of whether that first group exists as a readership at all is unclear. Adam Sol's *How a Poem Moves: A Field Guide for*

---

1. Share's "Poetry Makes Nothing Happen... Or Does It?" discusses Leighton's remarks on Auden's essay "The Public v. the Late Mr. William Butler Yeats", published in *Partisan Review* in 1939 (Vol. 6, No. 3).

2 See *Experimental Literature: A Collection of Statements*, edited by Jeffrey R. Di Leo and Warren Motte (2018), discussed in more detail in the second section.

Readers Afraid of Poetry (2019), meanwhile, is a book version of the project of explication that began with his blog; to its credit, it skips any definition of poetry or case for its importance. Instead, it states at the outset that, just as poetry matters to the author, "it probably matters to you; if you don't think poetry matters, you wouldn't have bought or borrowed or stolen this book". Sol's hermeneutic skill and passion are formidable, in whatever format they appear. But, when it comes to this pitch, I wonder what kind of patient, curious, yet entirely uninitiated reader might seek out such a book and benefit from it in the way Sol intends.

Matthew Zapruder's *Why Poetry* (2017) exists on a continuum with these gently proselytizing treatises, but it also gets somewhere different. Zapruder acknowledges the standard set of paradoxes outlined above while also bringing into sharper focus the much simpler and gratifying process of reading with care the actual words that make up a poem and, in doing so, "allowing one's imagination to adjust to the strangeness of what is there". Some of the book's most compelling moments draw on Zapruder's experiences teaching poetry. Take, for instance, his statements that "The portal to the strange is the literal", and that common classroom engagements with poetry—those attempts to decode the message in the mundanely disorienting text—miss the point that the most necessary tool for reading poetry is not some special spiritual insight or technical authority, but rather a dictionary. As this realization takes hold, Zapruder's students "remember that poetry is written in their language, and that all of us can be liberated into our own independent lives as readers". Zapruder recognizes its inherent worth in a way that underscores the engagement at the centre of poetry, not teaching as much as showing us that the engagement was already there: in moments we hated (more on this soon), or didn't get, or, most importantly, didn't acknowledge as engagement—as work—that had any value at all.

Compelling and entertaining as it is, however, Zapruder's argument is also familiar and tidy. His characteristically lucid and affirming statement that he is concerned with the "experience of getting close to the unsayable and feeling it, and how we are brought to that place beyond words by words themselves" is really just another description of the Romantic conception of the sublime—

that is to say, one more of poetry's paradoxes. TSusan Glickman
has described the sublime as a dynamic in which "nature ultimately
transcends translation into words, despite the fact that it is through
language that this failure of language can best be evoked"). Even
the outspoken Michael Lista, in the introductory essay in *Strike
Anywhere: Essays, Reviews, and Other Arsons* (2016), locates his ideas
about poetry in this familiar paradox. "Poetry is worth a damn
because it isn't good for anything", Lista writes, at times delving
further than most into the earthier details of its failures (with his
sniping at Canadian critics but, more universally and effectively, his
admission that "Poetry buckles under the weight of occasion, like
weddings and funerals, when most of us most frequently turn to
it for guidance and consolation"). Ultimately, though, Lista returns
to a genealogy of useful-because-useless tropes that stretches from
Keats to Auden to Marianne Moore.

The point of this book is not to repeat these tropes and
paradoxes, whatever multivalent and enduring truths are to be
found in them. Instead, I want to push past them. I argue that poetry
is useful in a practical sense. That is, the work of writing poetry is
work and produces more such work. Which is not to say that the
poet has direct control over the fruits of her labours or that writing
poetry thus allows us true self-determination and fulfillment.
Instead, I think poetry is useful because of its simultaneously
social and solitary act of creation and investigation—an act
that is fundamentally participatory and that breaks down the
oppositions, hierarchies, and distinctions that structure the poetic
paradoxes I've already outlined. Poetry absolutely does have
a readership, for example, even if those readers read it largely
because they want to write it. But is this really a bad thing? One
of the primary arguments I want to make here is that this form of
especially active reading-writing is—here's a paradox of my own—
inclusive precisely because of its gestures toward exclusivity. The
self-consciously elastic nature of this simultaneous welcoming
and retreating, I think, along with the multivalent relationships
between poetry and the semi- or unrelated working and political
lives most poetry people also commit to, sheds light on the
differences between work that is validating and work that doesn't
rise above drudgery, disingenuity, or exploitation.

My aim is to grapple with this sense of potential even when doing so reveals problems, or wrongheaded analyses, and—so often—lots of bad poetry. Doing so will involve going negative at times: perhaps unwisely, I'll take issue with Burt's didactically authoritative takes on contemporary American poetry yet again before this introduction is over. Relatedly, the can-we-write-bad-reviews debate in Canadian literary culture is over, or at least it should be for those who wish to live another day in CanLit— even I know better than to publish a true hatchet job. But I also don't believe that anyone who loves poetry really thinks that all reviews should be all positive, or generative, or whatever. There's a degree of disingenuousness in this element of the status quo. It's part of a larger, pervasive cynicism one finds in parts of poetry culture—something I'll be critiquing in these pages even as my larger claims are more affirming.

***

Making these arguments will require looking not only at the more accessible and even (yes!) popular aspects of contemporary Canadian poetry but, especially towards the end of the book, at more academically oriented areas of poetry culture. One finds in these spans of the poetry universe not so much inclusive claims for poetry's ongoing importance (like those of Burt and Zapruder) but more theoretically oriented attempts at making a case for poetry's political utility. There's a degree of overlap between these takes and arguments for the ongoing relevance of the avant-garde as a literary and artistic mode. As I'll argue in more specific contexts below, I think these err in the opposite direction of the all-affirming, feel-good takes—that is, they often force their observations into narrowly politicized or eccentrically arbitrary areas of inquiry. To draw from some recent such works that are poetry-adjacent, John Roberts' *Revolutionary Time and the Avant-Garde* (2015) seizes on "the technical challenges of art's post-art status" to argue that the avant-garde itself is useful as a "suspensive" category, in which the array of writers, writing, conferences, professorships, and networks that constitute the contemporary avant-garde have so successfully cleared a space for formal radicalism that even flagship avant-garde institutions (galleries, publishers, etc.) must struggle to "make sense of artistic change and stay in the game". Staying closer to poetry, Franco "Bifo" Berardi has argued recently in *Breathing: Chaos and Poetry* (2018) that the form, with its singular engagement with "words, sounds, and visual signs" provides an "ironic interrogation of Reality" and grounds us amid the chaos financial capitalism has wrought on whatever socio-cultural situation in which one finds oneself. It's this ability of poetry to provide rhythm through and in chaos that exists alongside and ultimately transcends the way poetry's "semiotic inflation" mirrors the economic phenomenon, or the way its imprecision and chaos mirrors that of the aging human brain.

These ideas are as compelling as they seem engineered to reflect their post-Berlusconi, Trumpian moment. It's a problem we find frequently in radical or experimentally oriented poetry criticism: the very specific conceptions of radicalism and activism that shape these inquiries also obscure the fact that lots of poetry doesn't do these things or concern itself with these contexts, even though it still might be doing something important. Roberts' compelling view of a varied and constantly changing mode of artistic production never seems convincingly political; it never really seems like there's this kind of avant-garde alternate reality or that the widely varied, ever-shifting swaths of the poetry world that wouldn't often be considered avant somehow can't do these things. And, to some extent, Berardi seems to be undercutting his argument by giving us a system of his own. Just as his wide-ranging take on poetry's singularity applies outside of the context of financial capitalism (a term that itself seems anachronistic considered from our deepening abyss of pandemic and climate-change hell), so do ideologically located readings of poetry often limit the multiple valences of the sui generis literary form. Narrowing our focus to Canadian poetry, many such critics and many contemporary writers who self-identify as belonging to the avant-garde often just want us to know how great their friends' work is—even when their work itself seems to have little in common with poetry that makes use of the practices often understood to constitute an avant-garde poetics.

***

Attempts to locate poetry in relation to pop culture, on the other hand—something else I'll address in the scattershot avant-and-beyond second half of the book—err by broadening the definition of poetry so far that, inevitably, we're talking about something else. Michael Robbins' *Equipment for Living: On Poetry and Pop Music* (2017), which I'll come back to in my essay on song lyrics, tries to discuss pop music and poetry as though they're the same. It lights on some interesting observations even as much of the book seems to reminisce about the equally slippery affective force of the sounds (not words) of classic and contemporary pop. The project Astro Poets, run by uniquely incisive American poets Alex Dimitrov and Dorothea Lasky, has found considerably more popularity. Sitting at 682 thousand followers as of this writing, the Astro Poets Twitter account has revealed a potentially productive linkage between poetry and astrology. The entity tweets brief, self-consciously poetic versions of the common astrological blurb. For example,

> Week of 11/29 in Sagittarius: It's time to ask for what you really want. You might not get it, but in the asking you will see what it is. If you can at dawn take note of the way there is always possibility. Wear the air of dreams as close as you can to the throat.

Capitalizing on the Twitter account's remarkable appeal, the project has since been spun off into a podcast and a book, *Astro Poets: Your Guides to the Zodiac* (2019). One gets the impression that the association, when written out at this length, may not get much deeper than superficial similarities. The book begins with an astute and promising connection of astrology with poetry:

> Every soul in the universe doesn't grow karmically in a systematic way, from one sign to the next, entering a "heaven" or whatever you want to call an afterlife. Existence is too complex for that. And astrology does not function as religions do. To the contrary, astrology provides many ways to think about living one's given life, and it's hard to know much about what happens after death (poetry might let you know that). It's our feeling that astrology is practical magic for your specific set of lifetimes. The karmic wheel is the spinning top along this twirling universe of possibilities.

While Lasky and Dimitrov follow through on this conceit insofar as every chapter ends with a poem in honour of the sign to which that section is devoted, the book falls short in that it doesn't really have that much to say about poetry. It's as if, having found validation in the connection of their craft with another of their long-term enthusiasms, the two ease into simply explaining to an ostensible readership of poets what the rules of this wacky zodiac are all about. By the time of the second chapter (on Taurus), one senses the anecdotes about celebrities and (less frequently) poets who share a particular sign giving way to the kind of "an Aries does x while a Taurus does y" analogies one might find in any astrological primer.

In other words, the book serves as a pop-culture-heavy astrology explainer with occasional mentions of poets and poetry. The result is the same: a promise to explore the workings of poetry turns out to be preoccupied instead with pedagogy, or paradox, or politics, or one's friends or one's hobbies. Do the poems themselves really not have anything to offer? I hope these pages suggest that they do.

***

To some extent, that's my approach: following the poems and considering where they take us. This kind of method (if it could even be called such) leads to the strongest moments of the above books about poetry's worth. Zapruder does something like this when he begins the second section of *Why Poetry* by referring to Marianne Moore's "Poetry". It starts off,

> I, too, dislike it: there are things that are important beyond all this fiddle. Reading it, however, with a perfect contempt for it, one discovers in it after all, a place for the genuine.

This dislike, shared by many who have approached poetry, in whatever context, is a key aspect of the dynamic Zapruder identifies when he stresses the need to avoid encountering poetry as a riddle to be solved. It's also what the Astro Poets get wrong when they treat poetry as an adjunct to astrology's not-bound-by-the-strictly-rational methods of making meaning. Poetry is in some ways parallel with this mode of apprehending and participating in the world, but it's also much more open to possibilities and ultimately more fulfilling—and, yes, more valuable.

The productive dislike Moore expresses in the form of a poem has also been used by Ben Lerner in *The Hatred of Poetry* (2016). Lerner refreshes the paradoxes of poetry in ways that bring us closer to my case for its practical value. He muses about what kind of art form "assumes the dislike of its audience and what kind of artist aligns herself with that dislike, even encourages it?" He provides familiar examples of the purported obsolescence or anachronism that is the contemporary poet—referring to those who are "foolish enough to tell another adult that you are (still!) a poet"—but also gives examples of the dual hatred and appeal that include would-be poets who submitted to a small magazine Lerner edited. This group included people with terminal illnesses as well as prisoners who were eager to assert their value as human beings, all of whom seemed not to regard it as a contradiction that they were "attempting to secure and preserve their personhood in a magazine that no one they know will see". Another of Lerner's seeming contradictions includes celebrated nineteenth-century poetaster William Topaz McGonagall, whom readers can almost universally recognize as poetically hopeless despite the ostensibly arcane nature of the artform that remains a mystery to Zapruder's uninitiated students. There are processes of exchange at work here—ones that share a dynamic of overcoming some impoverished earlier state. It's something that seems to go beyond the words themselves, although it's in those words that the process begins.

Lerner's conclusion combines these paradoxes. "All I ask the haters", he almost pleads, "is that they strive to perfect their contempt, even consider bringing it to bear on poems, where it will be deepened, not dispelled, and where, by creating a place for possibility and present absences (like unheard melodies), it might come to resemble love". I would add to this formulation that the work of perfecting one's contempt goes beyond just the reading of poetry, or the personal capacity for appreciation Lerner ends with. The point is that the paradoxes identify us and hail us, forming an almost religious contradiction in the sense that its value is in its secondary effect, of organizing life and giving us a model for working and producing and learning and interacting with others. And, because contemporary poetry can't ever be mainstream in a meaningful sense, it creates an affirmative sense of membership beyond just maybe sort of liking it—a membership that is at once active and constitutive yet relatively free from the harmful effects of those in-group/out-group dynamics that have become so pervasive since we started living online.

My own experience with poetry bears this out, revealing anecdotally something of the practical value I'm arguing exists despite poetry's reputation as frivolous, or at least unsystematized. However seemingly unnecessary or illogical to the outsider, there is a logic there in that poetry can function as the fibre holding together practical and social endeavours with intellectual engagement—a combination that comes naturally to some but often does not for people like me. I grew up in the kind of time and place where a family that was far from poor could accurately be described as working class in any other sense of the term. I vaguely recall some members of my family rolling their eyes at the idea of Canadian literature—maybe the concept of the arts in Canada generally, but Canadian poetry most certainly. When I was enrolling in university courses and found myself attracted to poetry courses anyway, the practice still felt like a joke or copout. I finished an Honour's Bachelor of Arts at the University of Toronto—the first person in my family to attain this level of education—and met the degree requirements with a grand total of one (1) course on Canadian poetry. After a year teaching English in South Korea, during which I read only the classic novels available at the two (2) English-language bookstores in town and roughly one-third of the collected poems of William Blake, I decided to put off further teacher training in favour of pursuing a master's degree. My statement of interest proclaimed my enduring interest in Canadian poetry, but by the time I was selecting courses, the entirety of the faculty's "vast range of Canadian poetry expertise" (my words from the statement) was either on leave or trying something else in the classroom. I ended up writing a Major Research Project (MRP) on Joseph Conrad and Wyndham Lewis. Poetry didn't pan out. That was fine.

Around this time, a friend shared an interest in Gwendolyn MacEwen. She stood out to me too in the few poetry-related classes I'd taken up to that point. I still like her. More than a few people have asked me why, and I'm still not sure I can answer the question. Because my less enlightened self mistook her low-stakes mysticism as the stuff of real poetry? (Sorry Zapruder—I was probably one of those students.) It may have been because she did have something of a system, and that it was located not only in her own interests and formal quirks but also in the larger localism of her Toronto-area exploits. I also came across some people who themselves liked her but weren't clear on why, just as I wasn't able to get too far into one of my favourite of her anthologized poems (which I failed to do anything notable with while teaching it during my doctoral studies several years later):

> This land like a mirror turns you inward
> And you become a forest in a furtive lake;
> The dark pines of your mind reach downward,
> You dream in the green of your time,
> Your memory is a row of sinking pines.
>
> Explorer, you tell yourself, this is not what you came for
> Although it is good here, and green;
> You had meant to move with a kind of largeness,
> You had planned a heavy grace, an anguished dream.
>
> But the dark pines of your mind dip deeper
> And you are sinking, sinking, sleeper
> In an elementary world;
> There is something down there and you want it told.

The turning inward establishes a theme of reflection and interior life from amid the long-clichéd wilderness of a *Survival*-style understanding of life in Canada. The idea was dated, in other words, and quite thin even compared to the thematic-criticism-by-numbers that characterizes much literary work from the period. And yet that thinness is at once excused and exposed by the sonic effects: the aural and visual resonances at the beginning of many lines (This / The / You / Your), half and pure rhymes at the end (inward / downward / time / pines), and the way these almost plodding resonances become still more incantatory pablum with the final stanza's "But the dark pines of your mind dip deeper / And you are sinking, sinking, sleeper". Okay, I finally have an answer. "Dark Pines Under Water" reads to me like it connects with the paradoxes I'm fascinated by but at this point also kind of impatient with. The poem possesses the knowledge about the literal and the ability of the literal to captivate, and for that reason it presents a system of circulation that's afloat precisely because of the lack of knowledge its function depends upon. To make further sense of it produces engagement, with the text and with each other, that at once exists for its own sake and yet is productive of something—even if that something can't always be grasped beyond the fact that it's productive of more engagement and more time spent.

This kind of knowing simplicity—the unadorned artifice that verges on whimsical—has informed other idealistic validations of poetry. The kind of productive engagement I'm arguing for might resonate, for example, with Georges Bataille's concept of expenditure. Different from the accumulation he saw as defining bourgeois life, expenditure is a form of non-productivity that stands in contrast to both a profligate bourgeoisie and a potentially magnanimous aristocracy.[3] Among these stark distinctions, the poet, with his twisted version of non-productivity—characterized by Bataille as "creation by means of loss"—neither accumulates nor provides for others. The poet, being "condemn[ed...] to the most disappointing forms of activity, to misery, to despair, to the pursuit of inconsistent shadows that provide nothing but vertigo or rage", either suffers in his embodiment of sacrifice or resorts to whatever degraded, "mediocre activity" finds the approval of bourgeois society. Nicholas Brown makes a more contemporary scholarly and Marxist argument: that the work of art in general is "not an archaic holdover but the internal, unemphatic other to capitalist society". Its unique ability is both to subject market desires to the analysis and explanation applied to other commodities while also standing outside this economy as singular objects of interpretation.

Brown's conception of the artwork appeals to me, but I don't think poetry specifically, at least as it is practiced today, is imbued with this pointedly economic or Marxian critical element. It's not

---

3   The essay also includes a larger opposition between this stratified society and a reductive understanding of the potlatch of various Northwest Coast Indigenous peoples as predicated on "humiliating, defying, and *obligating* a rival". See Bataille, "The Notion of Expenditure".

showing us what art might be if it were a commodity, but rather what work, in a positive sense, as severed from economic relationships, might yield in how we engage with the world, discursively and in a more practical sense. This may bear some relationship with activism, or what is sometimes described (in an increasingly cynical sense) as "organizing". But, as I'll get to in the following essay, the entire point of poetry is not to treat it as a convenient, easily graspable void into which the content of identity, political agitation, or some vague sense of justice can be placed. It's close engagement with the thing itself that is at once work, reward, and the means to a tangible creation of something that is at once community, skill set, and enactment of broadly humanist ideals. The result is that the practice of poetry shows us what work warrants its designation as such and thus has value regardless of the material worth of its product. In doing as much, it might also make clearer what kinds of work are subordinated to capital, or more directly exploitative, or just frivolous performance.

Nor do I regard poetry as an abstract reminder of how an entirely different society might have people use their excess time or energy, as Bataille does. But I do see a pervasive neoliberalism that has, in our daily practices if not our advantages and benefits, leveled the extreme stratification of the society he describes. And I see contemporary poetry as a form of expenditure that forges links among disparate practices and parties, sustaining a civil society of (mostly) good-faith engagement that resists value defined as monetary, based on an end product, or instrumental in that it is socially beneficial in some direct or predetermined way.

***

Parallel with my focus on poems rather than externally imposed systems, and with my own experience of poetry, I want to keep things a bit disparate in the pages that follow. In my years of 'sort of doing poetry'—reading, writing, reviewing, trying tangentially to make it my academic thing, failing—I have questions I can't really answer and ideas I can't really articulate. The goal of this book is to at once get a little deeper than asking "why poetry?" while also keeping a (somewhat) dispassionate distance, asking instead just *what* the thing is in its contemporary

Canadian context. Not the form itself, in an M. H. Abrams sense—there's little point in rehashing disciplinary and real-life consensus on the rough differences between poetry and prose. I mean instead the shifting, multiple, confounding, at once irrelevant and extremely relevant constellation of cultures, behaviours, and writing practices that make up the thing we're talking about when we talk about poetry here and now. In addition to this *what*, I'm interested in the *when*, the *where*, and the *for whom*. By which I mean not the nebulous debates over what being Canadian means or what Canadian literature more broadly was, is, or can be. What interests me more is the function of the thing that is contemporary poetry, as it plays out and is part of our cultural and intellectual life in the thing that the rest of the world knows as Canada.

A quite different approach—reading contemporary poetry's variety through the lens of external narratives and scholarly systems—also frequently comes up for critique in these essays. The academy has produced reliably sophisticated local readings and historical studies, but when it comes to the basics it seems woefully out of touch, or just unwilling to ask questions that matter. Case in point is Michael Robbins' "Ripostes", a 2013 review essay that argued the work collected in Paul Hoover's *Postmodern American Poetry: A Norton Anthology* continued to conceive of itself as somehow underground or unsung even as Hoover was forced to refer awkwardly to a major award doled out to one of its supposedly rebellious practitioners. (More on the Hoover fallacy later.)

This contradiction is at the heart of the idea that poetry is an eternal struggle between brave innovators and stodgy free-verse goofballs. Gregory Betts in has made a complaint that is similar to Robbins' but is about Canadian poetry, arguing in his essay "Before Our Time" that the idea of a literary radical presented in Pauline Butling and Susan Rudy's *Writing in Our Time: Canada's Radical Poetries in English (1957-2003)* has little in common with political radicalism. Betts takes the *TISH* writers as a case in point, seeing this group's enshrinement "into the mainstream body of Canadian literature" as contradicting any "rhetoric of antagonistic marginality". Butling and Rudy include in their list of supposedly radical poets anything-but-marginal writers like

Margaret Atwood, George Bowering, and Michael Ondaatje, whom Betts notes are "amongst the most taught, hired, awarded, and celebrated of contemporary Canadian authors".

Yet even Betts maintains stylistic divisions that separate them from more conventional twentieth-century writers: "What brings these writers together", he continues, is "their commitment to experimentation, to new poetics, and to literary innovation". The problem is that this appeared to be the shape of things in 2007, when Betts' essay was published. As a few have suggested since then, however, there is no longer as meaningful a difference between experimental and mainstream contemporary poetry. One might draw more extensively from historical avant-garde traditions than from the free verse that makes up the bulk of twentieth-century North American poetry. But avant-garde traditions are still traditions, and, despite those who insist that the avant-garde clique-bunker in which they hide their genius really does exist, the traditions they revere are increasingly found in all kinds of poetry—including that which reads on the surface like Al Purdy, or that written by poets not cool enough to be invited into the catacombs.

This false sense of a bifurcation, superimposed on the mass of everyone-doing-everything that contemporary poetry increasingly looks like, is similar to another overwrought controversy that attracts a lot of attention within the varied but in key respects unified contemporary poetry landscape: the now entirely mainstream preoccupation with identity. I would argue that this is increasingly becoming a kind of post-group identity in that it's based on individuals advocating for themselves as uniquely curated entities by locating themselves in increasingly complex, overlapping matrices of what we once regarded, and are still trained to regard, as group identities. Thinking of things in this way is, as many disgruntled thinkers have pointed out, a pretty new phenomenon. Kwame Anthony Appiah puts it refreshingly well when, early in his *The Lies that Bind: Rethinking Identity* (2018), he finds that, when Rosamond in *Middlemarch* "was almost losing the sense of her identity", it's because of new experiences affecting her emotional state. Identity is in this earlier sense "utterly particular and personal", but the term as it is currently used purportedly aligns us with "millions or billions of others". And yet, however skeptical we are, almost all of us keep in mind identity in its current usage when assembling a syllabus, journal issue, edited collection, or list of pretty much anything. I'll say more about this conflict in the essays that discuss, and, I hope, dismantle this and other limiting categorizations with which many conceive of twentieth-century and contemporary Canadian poetry.

If anything, it's the nebulousness of this poetry's making-nothing-happen forcefield that makes contemporary issues of identity and representation seem even more urgent, even more pushed to the foreground, here than anywhere else. Youth-oriented genres like Young Adult novels, comic books, and superhero movies tend to be more baldly didactic, of course. But my point is that poetry isn't about being educative—it's supposed to be about language, or nothing, or the opposite of both or either. The above paragraph notwithstanding, there won't be any anti-identity politics screeds in these pages. But I will say that I'm not interested in the concept of group identity as a meaningful strategy of categorizing contemporary poetry written in Canada. Part of the reason for this is that, as of the time of this writing, a conservative, white, straight, English-speaking male is no longer a default position but someone who is judged first and foremost according to his identity characteristics. The identity-based compartmentalization, like desperate binaries between experimental and mainstream as much as obsessively strict periodizations that can't account for the cusp figures or weirdos that make up so much of canonical literature, doesn't help us in determining what the form is or why it's churning away so furiously despite not mattering. And my use of the singular "it" is intentional—given the widespread nature of this generative dynamic, I choose in these pages to turn away from residual postmodernist orthodoxy and refer to *poetry* instead of a range of incomparable *poetries*.

Central to this conception of poetry are ideas of value and work, which I discuss in the following essay. In looking more closely at poetry's productivity and its lack of a market-identified product, I find not so much a utopian kind of production—in which something issues from labour and time that is distinctly our own—but instead a dynamic in which poetry can function as a form of value that is without any clear product beyond its existence as a record of research, or of work. It's processual and performative yet not directly connected to results, at least insofar as the latter are strictly defined or associated with a finished product. It keeps that product in mind, but it does so while indicating, in the form of possibilities that are separate from the latter, that our work—writing, discussion, interpretation, connection, engagement, introduction—matters in that our ideas and whatever other experiences are being processed themselves matter. It's for this reason that, as I'll discuss in the next essay, we sometimes encounter suggestions or implications that poetry, in not concretely mattering, must be used for something else (often political statement or more supposedly direct forms of activism).[4] But a more productive model, I think, is to comprehend through poetry this constellation of things it does do, and, in the process, to consider which kinds of work are meaningful and which are dehumanizing, redundant, or cynical.

Subsequent essays in the first section make related arguments about specific aspects of contemporary poetry culture. The first of these asks whether poetry reviewing (as opposed to literary criticism proper, with all its periodizations) might be better able to make sense of contemporary poetry's evolving and yet symbiotic relationships as they exist on the ground. The chapter suggests that, despite the personal politics of the genre, reviewing lets us acknowledge (however subtly) the realities of personal relationships, groupthink, grant-giving, fads, and the uncomfortable elements of the publishing zeitgeist that the hindsight of "literary criticism" proper seems so often to erase, or, depending on the distance, to be unaware of. By partaking in this present-relevance, whether that's literary-arts presentism or else being generative of "controversy" in challenging that presentism (an increasingly rare commodity), the capacious category of the review can be so much more than what is

---

4   The other side of this coin might be the work of some critics, discussed below, who have identified poetry as itself indicative of neoliberal containment: a miniature profession that drafts creative energy and supposedly free-bird sensibilities into a system of hierarchies and exploitation that isn't so different from—indeed, exists on a direct continuum with—the adjunctification of academic labour.

permitted by some contemporary understandings of the genre. With its potential for evaluation, tempered assessment, and, crucially, intellectual ambition in the form of rigorous scholarly engagement and poetic citizenship, the responsibly evaluative review as I understand it is more vital than any of the three archetypes of Canadian poetry reviewing—the positive, the negative, and the postmodern or experimental—might permit.

"I Just Wrote This Five Minutes Ago: Expectations, Originality, and the Contemporary North American Poetry Reading", takes as its title the frequent open-mic introductory comment—often made by a beginner or otherwise not really committed poetry writer—that seems to want to lower audience expectations even as it exults in the spontaneity that makes poetry as accessible as it is frequently denigrated by normies. The chapter tries to account for the quirks of the contemporary North American poetry reading, including several frustrations found recently in a cathartic Twitter thread—frustrations that included readers' declarations of the five-minute age of what they were about to read. Parsing these complaints reveals, on the one hand, that our preoccupation with the authenticity of the poetry reading has less to do with performance than with text-based notions of originality and craft. And yet, despite this preoccupation with the printed, and, one supposes, thought-about and edited poem object in its final form, the complaints suggest that the appeal of participating, or potentially participating, in the poetry reading requires that the craft remain free from the strictures of specialization.

The next essay, "Minimal Requirements", engages enduring conceptions of poetry as a minor form, or, paradoxically, the quintessentially minor form. It grapples with Deleuze and Guattari's politicized conception of minor literatures, finding a model that, with all its provocations, dissolves into a tangled, anachronistic mass of false oppositions. Meanwhile, some contemporary poetry— specifically, that which dwells on the tiny or the minimal, including in a physical, textual sense—responds to this paradox of centring oneself in the minor. With low stakes and low (or no) expectations, it creates the illusion of immensity; in doing so, it also captures the variety of contemporary poetry in a way that won't systemize it or smooth out its idiosyncrasies into clear stylistic or ideological contours. In this sense, the sampling of recent minimal-ish Canadian poetry I provide illustrates the cultural practices that make up the positive work of contemporary poetry.

Next, in "Formatting Engagement", I discuss the unique textual characteristics and distribution strategies of several small-press Canadian publishers, including Ottawa's above/ground press, London's Baseline Press, Toronto's Anstruther Press, and the North Vancouver-based Alfred Gustav Press. Considering these practices alongside the content of some of their recent publications, the essay argues that the intentionally obsolete formats or distribution methods behind these chapbooks are in fact far from indications of a subcultural myopia or boutique consumerism. Instead, I argue that this set of practices recalls past formats from a range of arts and deploys them so as to strengthen the back-and-forth of poetry's insider-outsider ecology.

This section closes with a look at the work of popular Instapoet Rupi Kaur. I regard Kaur less as a standalone success story than as a remarkable writer continuing a tradition of interpellative Canadian poetry—a tradition that includes Al Purdy and has a more recent iteration in the work of Billy-Ray Belcourt. This kind of poetry includes an educative element that, not always didactic in that it instructs on the level of content, is nevertheless welcoming on the level of form, format, and discourse more generally. It draws initiates into whatever space, sphere, or public is cleared by and for poetry and almost immediately hails those people into helping to hold that sphere together. While it's possible to take a cynical view of this phenomenon—that the body of reader-learners hailed by work like Kaur's is really being recruited as paying consumers of poetry, that a figure like Belcourt seeks to maintain his own institutional value, or that there's simply a narcissism in being a culturally validated pied piper—the larger result of this dynamic is the same kind of positive work and value that is produced via participation and supposedly frivolous expenditure. While not everyone who takes an interest in *Milk and Honey* will become a poet, or creative writing instructor, or bookmaker, they're engaging, and, regardless of exactly what that activity looks like, in doing so they're generating more engagement that isn't exactly the worst of its kind.

The second half of the book grapples with the persistent binaries and nebulous, collapsible notions of mode and genre that shape systematic attempts at understanding contemporary poetry's messy variety. The first essay, "On Formalism", unpacks and challenges a term in which nobody quite seems to believe and yet which plays a role in the binary and tripartite distinctions that structure so many poetry battles and readings of specific authors. In this essay I challenge conceptions of separately existing poetries that can only be taken on their own terms (according to some postmodernist critics and reviewers), finding instead a thread that links supposedly conventional verse with the work of two seemingly singular poets—Helen Hajnoczky and Moez Surani—whose work nevertheless is usually considered as belonging to Canadian poetry's experimental reaches. I find that commonly relied upon conceptions of craft, or the recognizably well-wrought poem, ought indeed to be regarded with suspicion. But my readings of these poets suggest as well that the term, with its evocation of attention, effort, and care, includes within itself a conception of our, and poetry's, limitations, and is for that reason useful in drawing attention to the value created by poetry. It's another paradox, but it helps us get past the clannishness that in this country continues to define much conversation about poetic form.

I then reheat a rivalry that appears to have cooled off in recent years—that between Montreal poetry mainstays Sina Queyras and Carmine Starnino—only to get away from the drama and into some of their poems. I originally carried out this comparative exercise (in the form of a conference presentation) to try to prove my suspicion that the supposedly intractable differences between the two had more to do with social (media) issues and the culture wars of the early to mid 2010s than with the poetry produced by either. I've found that not only is this in some ways the case, but that Starnino's much-discussed ideas about formalism aren't so different from Queyras' seemingly more expansive outline of poetic modes. The difference may be that Queyras benefits from presenting her ideas as more open to the world while Starnino's niche requires him, if mainly in a rhetorical sense, to challenge what he sees as outside his purview or interests.

The following two essays, "State of the Avant" and "Avant and the Future", confirm notions of the vitality of the contemporary avant-garde by insisting on challenging them. The first of these consists of a snapshot of a recent essayistic salvo that persists in considering the avant-garde as a distinct and inward-looking but somehow superior category. I try to determine exactly what's going on in the ostensibly hermetically sealed universe as some of its practitioners conceive of it, in the process finding an at times slavish traditionalism that, frustratingly and yet crucially, seems like it's all too aware of the paradox yet seems content to articulate it only indirectly. Accordingly, the essay that follows seeks a way out of the quagmire by looking at the supposedly cliquish functions of the avant. Along the way, it finds precisely the random contingency that makes the avant-garde both separate from and fundamentally a part of the dynamic I find in contemporary poetry generally.

In "What Were Lyrics", I then try to vindicate my takes on the practical importance of poetry by discussing a persistently frustrating area in which poetry and a distinctly different form are thought to overlap. My enthusiasm for poetry is younger than my interest in punk-related subgenres of popular music (many of which I want to call experimental but, in the spirit of my previous arguments, will not). Despite my ongoing investment in both poetry and pop, I'm not convinced that the two have that much in common, especially in their verbal aspects. I try to disentangle musical genres whose word-content might resemble poetry from that mass of radio sound that, at least in my view, does not exactly qualify as such. I also attempt to divide popular music lyrics into content and form, finding the stuff we call poetry approximated by the latter even, or especially, as we confront an absence of meaning, defined even in a loose, poetic sense. When lyrics become the manic, transfixed utterance of the identifiable, rhythmically defined persona, that's when they begin once again to converge with what we more frequently call poetry—even if the process depends on our reliance on a different kind of approximated content.

***

Finally, I hope these essays—and the voice in which they're written, not to mention the colloquial-clumsy phrasing of this book's title—make a point about the unique relationship between poetry and expertise. The same working-class person who half-thinkingly stumbled through poetry in the above anecdotes is also, for some reason, now writing a book about poetry that builds on years' worth of presentations, book reviews, and essays. Whatever authority I have or don't have, I hope that this strange book says something about "credentials"—about insiders and outsiders. I should state here that, while far from youthful, I'm by no means a veteran of the poetry wars. I came to the game late, for a variety of reasons. I also tend to be critical when it would be wiser to be agreeable. I come at the topic as someone who reads poetry, and to some extent writes poetry, but has also managed to keep it just on the margins of whatever is my "real" thing at the time—usually teaching and more properly academic publishing. I weigh in as someone who has, in the past fifteen years, read hundreds of collections of poetry, kept up with print and online issues of new journals, and practised literary criticism in both scholarly and reviewing contexts. Perhaps this peculiar position resonates with the elastic insider-outsider dynamics I find reproduced in contemporary poetry culture; perhaps it just means that I'm an unusually involved outsider, able to glance at the labyrinth from a little bit of a distance as opposed to from inside its walls.

I think this approach reflects the existence of a larger cultural milieu that is built on the dissolution and dispersal of the hierarchies of high and low culture, of course, but also the fact that everything, now, is to be interpreted and critiqued. At any suburban chain bar, one can hear by turns praise or pans concerning the representational equity of the latest superhero movie, as though these are first-order problems not only in the realm of pop culture but in a deadened, post-policy universe of Right and Wrong, of Good and Evil. Regardless of logical or analytical skills, everyone really is a critic. But not everyone is a poet.

One of the structuring features of contemporary poetry is that the bleeding hearts of the confessional open-mic scene coexist organically with the upper middle-class professional transgressors of the academy and institutional avant-garde. Burt's *Don't Read Poetry* (a 2019 volume similar in premise to the two mentioned above) makes this clear with a curious claim. Referring to Cortney Lamar Charleston's "Spell Check Questions the Validity of Black Life", with lines like

> **[Trayvon] Martin: did you mean traction?**
> Yes, in the way that lynching, the first
> quintessential American sport, has regained its
> footing among a younger generation—no robes
> worn, no fouls given, not a whistle to blow

Burt suggests that "Until recently (the form has other exponents now) nobody had written a smartphone-auto-correct poem, about Black Lives Matter or about anything else". When I read this, I knew something was wrong. While Burt doesn't claim precisely that this poem itself was the first published instance of the form, she goes some way in that direction. Which made me pause and think—yes, at that point many people had. Charleston's poem first appeared in the February 2015 issue of *Winter Tangerine Review* and was collected (with changes to the formatting and typeface) in *Telepathologies* (2017). And yet I know I've seen people do it at small-time poetry readings in Canada, including (as revealed by a glance at the list of poetry readings included on my CV) at least as early as the above poem's date of first. I'm sure I heard similar things much earlier, at those same Kingston open mics virtually nobody with Burt's pedigree has heard of or, if they had, would consider attending. I remember even then thinking at least one of these was incredibly predictable—pre-emptively clichéd?—and I remember discussing as much with my PhD supervisor (also not quite an avant-garde poetry insider) shortly afterwards. While it would have made sense to argue for the importance of the poem's combination of technology-based forms with the spoken-word style poetry that makes up the bulk of *Telepathologies*, positioning it as an absolute first of its kind—especially given the ubiquity of text-based jokes about autocorrect (themselves poems?)—seems overreaching and wrongheaded.

The point is that someone in Burt's position—that of a Harvard professor attempting to push into the mainstream as a politically correct poetry ambassador—has to be affirmative as opposed to critical. But—another paradox to add to the list—

evidently even she can't keep up with everything that's going on in contemporary North American poetry (something Burt acknowledges in the odd verb tense in which the above claim is constructed). This is likely because the poetry that becomes notable in a literary-historical sense will almost by definition be downstream from the poetry that few knew about (or, in the case of those innocuous autocorrect readings, even needed to know about). Contemporary poetry is what's happening around you, whether it's in a classroom, a new anthology, or a gathering at a small-town community centre.

This is probably also why those irritating, post-Great Recession (and, looking forward, probably post-COVID) takes on why poetry is "having a moment" seem so tone deaf. Take as emblematic here "Why Is Poetry Having a Moment?", a piece in which contributors from the London School of Economics chime in, giving a long view of poetry's increased popularity in times of crisis ranging from Italian city states, the Reformation, all the way through China during the World Wars. One contributor, International History professor Dina Gusejnova, suggests that "This is probably due to the fact that they are expected to speak truthfully and across boundaries to people living in societies which are split along competing lines of allegiance—to patrician families, to political parties, or to different mutually exclusive values". Gusejnova is right to point out that poets are "expected" to do such, but the rest of the feel-good roundup is less nuanced. What we get instead are reminders that in hard times people "need to feel an emotional connection" (Michal Nachmany, Grantham Research Institute on Climate Change and the Environment); that, in the era of fake news, poetry "can provide something genuine and considered" (Chris Redmond, poet); that an increased reach over social media and greater attention to diversity has made poetry "more relatable" (Angus Wrenn, Tutorial Fellow). But these reductive, wishy-washy characteristics disappear as soon as we look a little deeper: poetry as non-referential, explicitly or in terms of inscrutability; poetry defined as niche even while someone like Rupi Kaur amplifies that niche via Instagram and on into actual bestsellers; poetry as publicly relatable even while firmly in the realm of a twenty-year veteran tutorial leader at the

London School of Economics. All these forms of poetry are doing, or helping us do, something, but that something isn't the same as just making people feel a bit better during seemingly harder times.

The simultaneously existing frivolity and relatable vitality of the poetry world is evident when an effigy of these characteristics appears in the commentary of the non-literary world (often among writers carping about political correctness). It's as if they're peeking into a universe that's bizarre enough to provide the material for a few jokes but ultimately exemplary for the way its uselessness demonstrates the essence or furthest extent of some controversy du jour. Poets' purported lack of journalistic skill, or even basic linguistic competence, is a minor theme that appears when poetry-world blow-ups reach the outskirts of mainstream discourse. Both were in evidence in the petition that toppled the Poetry Foundation, which stated, "As poets, we recognize a piece of writing that meets the urgency of its time with the appropriate fire when we see it—and this is not it", only to then commit to its virtual page the words, "Given the stakes, which equate to no less than genocide against Black people, the watery vagaries of this statement are, ultimately, a violence". Science journalist Jesse Singal asked, in reference to this passage, "Do you guys think it's good or bad to have a definition of 'violence' that includes both 'Kneeling on someone's neck until you murder them' and 'Releasing a statement about someone's murder that lacks a certain...je ne sais quoi'?". But even this kind of snarky dismissal envisions a group with recognition, and with a Byzantine internal system of accolades and credibility, even if not everyone with a sinecure here is aware that vagaries doesn't mean the same thing as vagueness. The wholeness of that self-contained universe is invoked again by Jonathan Kay—no stranger to miscalculated sarcasm that verges on cruelty—when he writes in *Quillette* about the same episode, "'Until these demands are met,' the signatories warned readers, 'we will not be submitting any [poems] to the magazine'", ending with "The specified deadline is 'one week following receipt of this letter.' I don't want to alarm anyone, but that's tomorrow". Whatever you think of Kay, his remarks inadvertently show us that there's a kind of well-meaningness—a gentleness, maybe—in assuming that these things matter.

However much this sphere is mocked, it's also a robust and elastic place in which one tends to waste and unwaste time, often by working and not working. It's a space I occupy pretty frequently, like the time I was reading through Al Purdy's anthology, *Storm Warning 2* (1976), despite the fact that reading past the introduction, biographies, and notable selections wasn't entirely necessary for the project I was working on. I came across one Andrew Wreggitt, whose bio read, "Born Sudbury, Ont., 1955. 'Anything else of relevance which does not appear in my poetry, does not exist.' Lives in Fraser Lake, BC".

Wreggitt contributes the poems "On Wasting Time" and "On Summer". "On Wasting Time", especially, is interesting enough to distract me for a while longer. What happened to this poem? But first—what happened to Wreggitt? Google shows me a personal website, which reveals that in addition to five books of poetry, he wrote five plays and "more than 90 hours of produced network television", including for 1990s TV series *North of 60*. At the height of the pandemic in Ontario, I search for his debut collection, *Riding to Nicola Country* (1981), on Worldcat and find about two-dozen physically existing copies, inaccessible to me and yet spread around central Canada, the US, and beyond. Worldcat lists the book on Harbour Publishing, but my search of that website yields nothing. Wreggitt's website says it was published by Saskatoon's Thistledown Press—which is still active, even if a search of its website also turns up nothing under his name.

I try not to order books from Amazon, but, given the circumstances, I break the rule and find copies of two of Wreggitt's subsequent books, *Man at Stellaco River* (Thistledown, 1984, this copy once the property of University of Waterloo Library) and *Zhivago's Fire* (also Thistledown, 1997, this one formerly of Edmonton Public Library). When they arrive, I open the first and browse the table of contents... not what I'm looking for. I start reading it anyway (like what happened with *Storm Warning*) and find a voice similar to the one that caught my attention in "On Wasting Time". But it's diluted in more by-the-numbers lyric CanPo from the 1980s. The first section of the book includes "Daniel Harmon: A Geography", which traces the westward journey and related exploits of the early nineteenth-century fur trader. All of which is to say that the book's strongest points are only somewhat interesting. (Indeed, a contemporary review of *Riding to Nicola Country*, addressed by Douglas Daymond along with nine [!] other poetry titles in *Canadian Literature*, opens the omnibus piece by describing all the poetry concerned as "neither abysmally bad nor startlingly good". Apparently, Wreggitt's debut includes "[d]espair, violence, and physical or mental suffering" as opposed to the more cavalier matter of the poem I want to find, "On Wasting Time". Daymond says it shows "too little variation in tone" despite some "precise and engaging" poems). Like many things in 2020, the story staggered to a non-conclusion when I went to the Toronto Reference Library in the earlier days of the first mismanaged reopening, in search of *Riding to Nicola Country* (university libraries still being closed). After struggling to find somewhere to get a coffee, sitting down and remaining fully masked, and opening a copy of the thirty-nine-page debut, I found that—oh good!—"On Wasting Time" was absent from the table of contents. I quickly read it through, finding a decent dose of despair, violence, and suffering, but not my poem, nor anything like an alternate version. The poem seems never to have found a more permanent home than the anthology, making it a footnote— and my discovery of that fact should be a footnote in this book, but for the next development in the story.

Although in a hurry (not wanting to stay indoors for long, also needing to check a few other references in texts on the shelves), I took a quick look *Southeasterly* (1987), another of Wreggitt's collections on the shelf. No sign of my poem! Could I justify sitting there longer with the book, an afternoon appointment looming? No, but I took pictures of its pages just in case. The next day, frustrated, procrastinating, and aimless, I used spare moments to read these poems. After reading each two-page set, I deleted the series of photos. Wreggitt would have run into trouble today, I noted, deploying Indigenous themes using a Purdy-esque free verse—a style I'd describe, in the spirit of Daymond, as neither abysmally bad nor startlingly anything at all.

What has been gained? All my photos deleted, I'm left with the half-knowledge that "On Wasting Time" is the work of the same Wreggitt behind *Man at Stellaco River* and *Southeasterly*, and yet it's just otherwise enough to be notable—it has the same flat, easy style but with a quicker turn to self-deprecation, a more flippant choosing and then casting aside of metaphor and allusion, a little more rigorous use of half-rhyme and consonance. In other words, it's a little more aware of just how much the work behind the poem is worth. The frivolous task of looking for its other incarnations was onerous and futile given the evolving shutdown and reopening regulations that characterized the summer and early fall of 2020 in Ontario. For a reason that lies at the heart of this book—the slight improvement of an obscure poet signalling that even marginal progress can be noticed by similarly obscure readers, that doing this work is not wasting time for no reason, but for a good reason—reproducing the poem as a whole allows it to be read by those who perhaps wouldn't otherwise be able to, even if they for some reason knew of its existence. This instance of my wasting time with poetry may produce value for you, which would make it time that was wasted productively. If it still matters—and I think it does—here it is:

ON WASTING TIME

I have watched two little girls
brush each other's hair
in the hot sultry blue sky of afternoon
I have spit into the Bow River
expecting its metabolism to change
I have beer-pissed over a cliff
feeling like a Goliath
with the power of rivers at my fingertips
I have walked in peace marches
and been completely fooled by politics
I have written poems that I thought were important
and generally have completely wasted my time
doing things that don't matter to anyone
even me

But I do them anyway
I mean, Alexander the Great
wasted his time conquering Persia
and died of a stupid fever
while the Persians just took over again anyhow
and my father spent his life

doing nearly everything under the sun
and accomplishing almost nothing

I don't feel bad about wasting my time
eating blades of grass under a tree
or writing volumes of poetry
or not having the energy to sit in the sun
and get tanned
because no one really cares
if my father conquered Persia
or if I threw up from eating too much grass
or if the two little girls
stopped brushing their hair and grew up
The Bow River didn't turn into spit
so let's not get fanatical
over a few moments of wasted time
(if such a concept exists)
I mean it's all relative to
the price of oats in Bolivia
and the circumference of my love
(by which I mean nothing at all)
like wasting time
I mean, if I think I'm Goliath
or if I really am
doesn't matter

In the Siamese kinship
of wasting and non-wasting time
this poem has no end
Imagine it, if you like
disappearing into the sunset
mumbling
nothing
at the blistering of sun
and bearing noisy witness
to wasting time

Part 1
WORKING POETRY CLASS

Make Work Mean

Despite the nothing it does or doesn't make happen, poetry is at least around. It functions within whatever kind of irrelevance one might attribute to it. Although it's nowhere near as omnipresent as music, poetry is nevertheless woven in the fabric of our culture industries, our education system, as well as many people's conceptions of vocation and even self. That said, as I try to make the case for the practical value of reading and writing poetry, I'll turn now to the thorny question of what poetry—poems themselves and the whole mass of overlapping cultures, processes, and personas we refer to when we say the word *poetry*—actually does.

I also consider how poetry's *something* (or absence of anything) fits in with the semi- or unrelated working lives most people who are involved with poetry must commit to. Following the premise that poetry itself makes/is nothing to its most cynical endpoint—and taking into account as well the fact that various forms of labour pervade all aspects of our current lives, at all times, unlike many of the temporally compartmentalized activities that still come to mind when we hear terms like *work*—this essay asks what poetry about work actually looks like and does. Is poetry itself valuable as work? If not, must poetry, then, be or do something else? Something more recognizable as work that creates value or produces some identifiable change in the world? It seems like some people think so. But, as I'll argue here—

after offering some examples of recent poetic engagements with work as traditional forms of production, as poetic considerations of such, and as insistences that poetry itself must be or do something concretely useful—I think a more productive model is provided by poets and poems that are cognizant of these systems but also conscious of poetry's status just outside them. As seen in Catriona Wright's *Table Manners*, with which I'll conclude, I think poetry has an important role to play in dramatizing the distinction between labour that has value and that which is merely dehumanizing in its redundancy. And, in turn, in showing us what a productive poetic engagement with work might look like.

Work's Aesthetic Residue

A commonly cited labour-centric Canadian poet is Tom Wayman, and a classic example of what might be regarded as a traditional engagement with the topic comes with "Factory Time". From *Free Time: Industrial Poems* (1977), "Factory Time" registers the way the cyclicality of the old-fashioned, straightforwardly defined workday leaves a mark on us even when we're off the clock. The poem begins by breaking down the timeline of a shift: "The day divides neatly into four parts / marked off by the breaks. The first quarter / is a full two hours, 7:30 to 9:30". But it quickly challenges this uniform notion of time, qualifying its early description with the statement that the full two hours of work is "okay / in theory, because I'm supposed to be fresh, but in fact / after some evenings it's a long first two hours". The obsessive calculations throughout the poem—"only 110 minutes. / Also, 20 to 30 minutes before the end I stop / and push a broom around"— give way to a sense of being permanently on the clock, the poem stating, "But even when I quit / the numbers of the minutes and hours from this shift stick with me", and then concluding with a robot-like performance of always being on:

> and the automatic computer in my head
> starts to type out: *20 minutes to 9, that means
> 30 minutes to work after 9; you are
> 50 minutes from the break; 50 minutes
> of work, and it is only morning, and it is only
> Monday, you poor dumb bastard ...*

4

Wayman looks forward to our current reality of ever-collapsing boundaries between work and play. Even as we navigate this change in the third decade of the twenty-first century, the shift from what we would now regard as the old-fashioned work of the factory floor, something that, even if it seemed crushing at the time (Wayman's "Overtime", from the same collection, almost dutifully laments having "two hours out of the whole day / to do what I want for myself, / which usually turns out to be nothing, since the time is so short"), is in the neoliberal era revealed as a relatively simple division of time in which there was comparative freedom.

If we jump forward in time quite a way, we can see the sort of neoliberal reality zoo Wayman might have been anticipating. But it requires a few shifts in gear to get to any poetry-centric theorizations of this world. A particularly compelling formulation departs from lyric and anything like manual labour to engage with the world of high art and the Language writing from which Wayman's work became increasingly estranged. Felix Bernstein's *Notes on Post-Conceptual Poetry* (2015) argues that conceptual writing privileges the curatorial and fashionable as opposed to the intellectual, thus "reorganiz[ing] the boundaries that separate work from play, art from life". Never straying far from Pierre Bourdieu's conception of the mutually reinforcing forms of capital that structure our lives,[1] Bernstein comments on the ideology underneath New York City's poetry and visual-art worlds. He distinguishes earlier, more self-serious forms of conceptualism from what he calls post-conceptual poetry, which "attempts to explicitly bring affect, emotion, and ego back into the empty networking structures that govern us". Despite its grounding in liberatory theory and aesthetics, the reintroduction of these idiosyncrasies is essentially neoliberal and self-serving (as indicated as well in what David Balzer has described as the ascendancy of the curator in the contemporary

---

1   Bourdieu's influential conception of the interdependence of economic capital and the less tangible forms of cultural and social capital first appeared in English in "The Forms of Capital" (1986).

art world more broadly).[2] In this post-conceptual reality, all aspects of our emotional, private, social, and working lives are material that is arranged by the poet, out of which her curatorial brand emerges.

But neither is Wayman some procrustean working man of yore. "Tool Fondle", also from *Free Time*, anticipates other shifts in the way work works: between working time on the clock and off, between manufacturing and services, and also between conceptions of lyric poetry as separate from work and its imbrication with the other forms of labour that fill our days. The poem begins with an almost fetishistic description of the speaker's tool set: "These are of dull or silvery metal. Then there are colors: / the yellow plastic handles of my assorted screwdrivers, / the deep luminous blue of the 3/8ths nutdriver handle". His tools are valorized for the "real work" they allowed the speaker to do—"And with all these, I built more than a thousand trucks"—but also as consumer objects, with the set already personalized through years of use and yet, by the end of a poem in which manual labour has for the speaker been succeeded by a routine in which "I've gone back to writing things down / on a typewriter", further curated for the sake of nostalgia: "I always meant to get a good vicegrip / and a file. Maybe I'll go downtown tomorrow / and see what they're asking". The implements of work have here become curios, in the process generating work of a different kind.

Vanessa Place and Robert Fitterman delve deeper into how remunerative work among this milieu doubles as the source material for artistic production. Specifically, they implicate the "repressive market economy" from which "there is no escape" and which "will banalize and commodify any mass attempt at subversion" in the development of conceptual writing, mentioning poetry constructed from search-engine inquiries as an example of writing that reflects the totality of market

---

2   Balzer argues that "curationism"—"the acceleration of the curatorial impulse to become a dominant way of thinking and being"—has, since the mid-1990s, created a scenario in which "institutions and businesses rely on others, often variously credentialed experts, to cultivate and organize things in an expression-cum-assurance of value and an attempt to make affiliations with, and to court, various audiences and consumers".

relations. But they also take a more general view of this totality when they draw on Sianne Ngai's conception of the zany, an aesthetic category Ngai describes as "turning the worker's beset, precarious condition into a spectacle for our entertainment". Place and Fitterman unpack the (since the time of their writing, even more ubiquitous) "perk" of working remotely, which, as it has become more widespread, has obscured the distinction between work and leisure; this "perverse fulfillment of the socialist promise that labor, not leisure, will be the source of self-realization" is encapsulated in newly allegorical writing such as the above example, in which received experimentalist methods express "the conflation of work (research) and play (composing)".

We're always on, and our very production of poetry, at least if we're publishing it and using it to navigate the artistic and professional milieux with which it shares space, reflects as much. (Think of the graduate student who has forsaken music for NPR, or the more classical image of the poet-diarist-artiste taking notes.) But does poetry lead us to something positive in both cases? What, exactly, is affirming about the work documented, poetry's documentation of it, and our grappling with the documentation of the documentation? This kind of meta-literary compoundedness used to seem frivolous, but now it strikes me as something else. In keeping with Zapruder's advice to stay as close as possible to the actual words, I'll look in this chapter at more poems that are about work in its various forms. But to clear the way for that, I'll take the opposite route and explore a jarring example of the idea that poetry really may not be anything at all—that it, by extension, must be an empty vessel for carrying something else.

An Empty Vessel Must Carry Something Else

The Covid-19 pandemic didn't have to rage for too long before the fallout hit poetry. Or, more accurately, before poetry, with nothing of its own to do, became a libidinal and yet contrarian prism through which the fear, anxiety and outrage that defined North Americans' fumbling response to a public-health crisis were refracted and refocused yet one more time. For me, the pandemic started in Wuhan, China, which I left for my vacation a couple weeks before the crisis became apparent. I came back from Southeast Asia through a different part of China as things were starting to unravel, various restrictions encompassing more of Hubei province and warnings sounding abroad as the virus extended its reach. Shortly after I met a friend in Macau, Wuhan was fully locked down. I thought about returning to another mainland province and waiting for the lockdown to lift, but at this time I was hearing stories about Hubei residents (both Chinese and foreign) being denied accommodation and otherwise being discriminated against in other parts of the country. So I flew to Manila, where I was marooned for a couple weeks due to newly imposed travel restrictions on the part of both China and the United States. When it became obvious that the quick improvement many had hoped for wouldn't come, I gave up and returned to Canada. I was able to attend a poetry chapbook launch in Toronto, right around the time larger and university-sponsored poetry events were starting to be cancelled. Two days later, Ontario's first set of closures was announced.

It's from this perspective that I watched the fallout. First, around the time China had eliminated the virus, there was a brief cathartic outburst of nationalism and xenophobia, reportedly directed in some places at residents of African descent, but, in terms of overall sentiment, at foreigners in general (and, for obvious reasons, Americans and Japanese especially). This was around the same time that various outlets circulated a rumour that the disease had come not from animals somewhere in the Wuhan area but rather from the American military, whose delegation to the World Military Games (held in the city the previous October) had deliberately planted the virus in an act of biological warfare.

I spent a little while wondering how anyone could believe such a thing, or why a society could explode into hatred of the other in response to a domestic problem. I didn't have to wait long for an answer. As pretty much anyone reading this will remember, the severity with which most Western countries bungled their responses to the pandemic soon became clear. In the United States particularly, nearly a thousand people were dying of the disease every day. And yet the object of many Americans' building ire was not the virus, nor the Trump administration's inept and careless response, but systemic racism in policing—something as unrelated to these issues as Africans, Americans, or the Japanese were to China's early-2020 epidemic.[3] Following the same logic, in the middle of a once-in-a-century pandemic, amid a newly entrenched Cold War, and following a particularly cruel and shameful instance of police brutality, what better institution to attack than the Poetry Foundation?

The incident as most (of the poets reading this) will recognize it began with the statement the Poetry Foundation made on June 3rd: that it stood in solidarity with the Black community on issues like the one that led to Floyd's murder. The statement was deemed inadequate by enough *Poetry* contributors and award winners that an open letter, attributed to Fellows + Programmatic Partners of the foundation, was posted on June 6th; the signatories asked that the lack of "details, action plans, or concrete commitments" in the original statement be rectified by actions such as the replacement of the foundation's president, the composition of a more meaningful statement outlining the ways in which it would fight racism, an acknowledgement of the debt the foundation owes to Black poets and those of other identity groups, and the redistribution of the institution's wealth and related opportunities to the aforementioned identity groups.[4]

On one level, the revolt may not say that much about poetry. It could be another example of activist culture struggling to define itself at a time when its most popular causes have been paid lip service by the largest corporations in the world. Similarly, and still more cynically, the exercise could well have been the same type of dynamic that has always obtained among A-types in the liberal professions and fine arts—to position oneself as a rebel and outsider just enough to mark one's ascendance into

3   Given that racialized people have been overrepresented in the US and Canada in terms of case numbers, and have suffered greater rates of mortality, the attention to systemic racism made somewhat more sense than did generalized xenophobia. Yet the response still resulted in activities that directly contravened pandemic containment.

4   The letter was accessible on google docs at the time of writing, but is no longer available.

the supposedly oppressive and stifling halls of power. Still, the dynamic I'm more interested in—what kind of work poetry is and does—is visible to me in the original letter and, to an even greater degree, some alternate versions of the petition that circulated online in early June.

In fact, petitions and open letters were already making the rounds beginning in late April, in response to the foundation's statement on the 23rd that it remained committed to its programs and financial support for poets but that the "unprecedented challenges due to COVID-19" meant that there would be a "significant immediate impact and unknown long-term impact" on the value of its endowment.[5] For example, speCt! Books, an Oakland-based chapbook publisher, took issue with the idea that the foundation's finances were in any way precarious; they published a change.org petition, as well as an open letter of their own, in response.[6] This statement consisted of two "suggestions". The first was a naïve attempt to claim that no such financial instability could possibly exist (based on the observation that "the stock market" was worth as much on April 27, 2020, as it was at the end of 2017), and that therefore the Poetry Foundation very much would be able to make new commitments to their community. The second demanded more transparency with their financial situation, pointing out the exorbitant salaries paid to the foundation's President and CFO (Henry Bienen and Caren Skoulas, respectively). speCt!'s change.org petition was updated following Floyd's murder to demand, among other things, Bienen's immediate resignation—owing to his past work as an analyst for the CIA during the first Cold War—and the assembly of a new, majority POC board.

The most extreme iteration of these statements that came to my attention synthesized the above objections into a series of demands that get to the very crux of what poetry is, or isn't, or ought to be. This was something called the PoFo Boycott Letter, put together and circulated on Twitter by someone named "z howslee"

---

5   See "Poetry Foundation on COVID-19 Relief."

6   See speCt! books, "Tell the Poetry Foundation to be Accountable to Its Community" and "An open letter to the Poetry Foundation regarding their COVID-19 Response Statement."

(@sweatybikeman, although as of this writing the account has been deactivated).[7] The demands were divided into categories of immediate, short-term, and long-term. Immediate demands included redistributing "cash on hand to black liberation work **immediately** [bold face in original], including contributions to groups engaged in black liberation work as well as unconditional cash transfers to black poets" as well as converting the Loop Chicago building into "a gathering center and sanctuary for those engaged in the current uprising". The latter idea found expression as well in the list of short-term demands—"the swift distribution of reparations" in the form of "unconditional cash transfers" to "those directly and indirectly harmed by the work of the Poetry Foundation and Eli Lilly, including prisoners and diabetics" as well as to "poets in need during the current pandemic and attendant economic crisis", with a list of designated groups in which "Native and Black writers" were to be prioritized. Long-term demands, in addition to repeating the idea about cash distribution, mentioned the need to "[r]econfigure the Poetry Foundation's role in the poetry world from its current status as a wealthy kingmaker to a platform for resource distribution, with a particular emphasis on redistributing resources to poets in the greatest position of need" and to "[c]onvert the downtown Chicago space into a hub for radical political organizing, resource center, and free lending library".

While I like the idea of expanding lending libraries, I think the demands I've highlighted are notable for their idealism as well as their cynicism: it's hard to ignore that the most materially and monetarily useless of forms was deemed a logical candidate to supply such immediate, tangible, tactical assistance to an ongoing protest movement. In their quest to achieve real-world political change, the poetry community focused on a poetry institution that actually did very little to advance interest in the form that supposedly does nothing. The logic of cause and effect isn't there; instead, it's as if the very physical manifestations of poetry were to be razed, converted into pure spatial and monetary assistance

---

7   I'm working from a copy of the letter I made on 5 June 2020; the Google Doc is still up as of this writing, but those who wish to read it must request access: https://docs.google.com/document/d/15erF4gp2v4lHvH2_HTO4spdaRGYpgBKskbHXMeBAQww/.

for an ideological cause. As far as I know, few of the poets joining this cause have circulated petitions demanding that Halliburton, or the US Military, or Republican state houses and political offices liquidate themselves in this way, despite the fact that all of them, it should be uncontroversial to remark, do far more damage to marginalized people than does the Poetry Foundation. Perhaps the distinction is simply tactical—of course an arts institution would be more likely to give in to such demands than would any component of the US military-industrial complex. But it's hard not to see this as scapegoating, given especially that all of it was happening in the midst of a literal pandemic under which Americans—and especially Americans marginalized by race, sex, gender, disability, and class—had every reason to feel powerless.

This is emphatically not to state that there is no room for politics, implicit or explicit, in poetry. Just the opposite, I think—it's hard not to get the impression that poetry worth reading usually has some topical relevance or political valence. Shortly before @sweatybikeman tried to set the world on fire, I spent $30 on a great pandemic marketing initiative—a box of roughly fifty backlist titles from a prominent publisher of Canadian poetry. The box included exactly what one would expect—a few hits, a few more misses, and a lot in between, including a lot that I wouldn't have read had I not been stuck inside with the big book box. One title stood out to me because of its paratext, which consisted of surrealist whimsies so innocuous as to make one wonder if the author, wherever they were, had circa mid-2020 even heard of either Floyd or the pandemic. The lines that really got me—"What if Nick Drake and Emily Dickinson met in the afterlife? What if a respected physician suddenly shrank to the size of a pea? What if the blind twins in a Victorian photograph could speak to us? What if we found another Earth orbiting another sun?"—make me wonder whether poetry that matters must, by definition, combine its refinement of uselessness with something we can grasp on to as somehow vital and present.

A Vessel for Itself
Combining the useless with the ostensibly useful, even as poetry is suspended from the truly practical, isn't an impossible

balance to strike. Poetic language itself, after all, construes authenticity as artifice. Fittingly, to find an example of that elemental duality in Canadian poetry, one need look no further than the quintessential CanPo everyman, Al Purdy. Artifice is at the heart of Purdy's workmanlike persona, whether it's the remunerative employment boasted about in his work poems or the work of writing the poems that would supersede the manual labour that sometimes furnished their content. Purdy, as denigrated as he's been for his supposedly simple, Canadian-sounding free verse, is an example of a poet whose writing refers to and is at times structured by the labours of his day-to-day life.

Among other manual-labour jobs, Purdy worked in a mattress factory in Montreal. One of his notable later poems recounts his time at an even less savoury occupation: stacking bags of powdered blood. "Piling Blood" begins by describing the task at hand: "It was powdered blood / in heavy brown paper bags / supposed to be strong enough / to prevent the stuff from escaping / but didn't". The stanza pattern recreates the rhythm of a shift, with the next section reiterating the previous description and shifting focus from things to actions: "We piled it ten feet high / right to the shed roof". The next, beginning,

> I forgot to say
> the blood was cattle blood
> horses sheep and cows
> to be used for fertilizer
>
> the foreman said[,]

subordinates narrative structure to the demands of the task, complete with interruptions and disjointed conversations spread across isolated moments. And despite Purdy's purported formal slackness, the poem's movement from line to line mirrors the physicality of putting down one bag, then another, the above lines ending in consonant-heavy monosyllables (say / blood / cows / said) with *fertilizer*'s odd four-syllable finish slumping awkwardly amid all the thudding. This is work poetry that puts us inside the task, and, in repeating the raw, repetitive movements of some kinds of labour, construes poetry itself as work. And all this leaves aside the poem's grisly content—Purdy's nondescript statements render the grotesque, mechanized treatment of animal life as just more of the stuff that gets our hands dirty, thus pointing to the invisibility of this suffering. The scene itself is topical and political.

However real his work writing may have been, Purdy didn't continue working such jobs once he'd found ways for poetry to sustain him. And while he may have mocked academia, Purdy also, as discovered by Ernestine Lahey, made a serious attempt in the 1960s to gain admission to York University as a mature student. Lahey acknowledges that this effort (documented in 1964 correspondence between York and Purdy as well as a reference letter from written by *Tamarack Review* editor Robert Weaver) may have been evidence of insecurity. Regardless, one finds in the endeavour yet another example of the interweaving of work, art, and artifice that characterizes Purdy's poems. It's this tapestry that is present even in the most caricatured aspects of Purdy, encapsulated in the 2015 film, *Al Purdy Was Here*, and random YouTube snippets used to introduce the now less-than-shocking figure in undergraduate classrooms. Mark Silverberg has deconstructed this "robust," typically working-class Canadian persona, arguing that the literary establishment of the mid to late twentieth century, in "reductively Canadianizing" Purdy, has obscured the nuances of the man himself as well as his work. But that Canadianization itself, however inaccurately it captures the essence of any actual Canadian, might say something valuable about the contradictions that make Purdy Purdy, and Purdy's poetry valuable as poetry.

This compulsive oscillation between concealing and revealing his erudition is part of the duality of authentic and artsy-fartsy that defines Purdy: his writing is fused with his "real" work and, eventually, becomes his work. The dynamic brings to mind Richard Sennett's conception of craft as involving an "intimate connection between hand and head":

> Every good craftsman conducts a dialogue between concrete practices and between problem solving and problem finding. The relation between hand and head appears in domains seemingly as different as bricklaying, cooking, designing a playground, or playing the cello—but all these practices can misfire or fail to ripen. There is nothing inevitable about becoming skilled, just as there is nothing mindlessly mechanical about technique itself.

Purdy does this in that he writes almost the same poem again and again and again (starting with the thousands of bad poems, in draft, journal, and manuscript format, that purportedly survive at the University of Saskatchewan Archives and Special Collections). He wrote poems like he made parts of mattresses—when he had to. It's just that having to write poems occurred off the clock, and so more frequently.

Purdy's high output and easy lyric style has earned him the scorn of formally minded poets and critics. I've written elsewhere that there is a certain attention to form in Purdy—a subtle formalism that exists precisely because it is intuitive. I would add here that Purdy's workmanlike poem-production adds a further dimension to his poetics. Not only is Purdy learning his craft in the gaps between his working life proper and in its aftermath, but the reams of poetry that result document exactly the kind of long-term process Sennett describes. It's hard to conceive of this kind of poetry as so frivolous that it ought to be vaporized, its energy somehow captured and reconstituted so that it supports what at some given moment is deemed by a critical mass of literary people to be a worthy political cause. Even a stylistically middle-of-the-road, frequently maligned poet like Purdy can do important work with his poetry, using it to document, supplement, consider, and transform whatever kinds of labour filled his other hours.

What Work We Might Do

Of course, Purdy's grappling with the work of poetry might not be so useful a model going forward given that we no longer live in Purdy's world. Instead, we face precarious employment and the near-total collapse of the structured clock time that Wayman merely suggests might be destabilized. We organize our time instead to make sure that we're advocating for ourselves in a range of social and professional fields. If all we do is increasingly some kind of work—including the artifice of forming and performing a suitable persona—what does poetry about work look like? Are the two the same? If so, is voiding the poetry itself, or transposing it into the social work of activism, in fact the logical and responsible way of grappling with these shifts in how we use our time?

Byung-Chul Han's *Burnout Society* (2015) provides an interesting account of what makes our times unique. The book is a short, handily topical look at the burnout that results from our hyperconnected world. But its grand strokes also show us a way forward via a positive poetry of work. Specifically, Han gives us a way to see when craft and the stylistic affinities associated with it represent a meaningful individualistic engagement with an art form—a combination of similarity and difference that represents some actual experience and understanding of the world represented—versus when they illustrate only a sense of craft that can be reduced to rote activity or busy work. He describes the shift from what he calls an "immunological age", in which threats come from outside the body or self, to the "massification of the positive" that defines our present moment. In this new totality, or "[a]chievement society", our difficulties are the result not of disciplinary prohibitions and directives but of a sense of "[u]nlimited Can" defined by "projects, initiatives, and motivation". The response to this condition of undifferentiated work-life is a kind of "hyperactivity, hysterical work, and production", or a society of work that constructs us as "laboring slave[s]".

Han's analysis is marred by distasteful language: he equates those suffering from various burnout-related mental-health afflictions with the emaciated prisoners of concentration camps; at another point he refers to the autism of the "idiot savant". But his descriptions of the burned-out subject as having a weakened capacity for negative feelings like dread or mourning are valuable for their articulation of a state in which thought is transformed into mere calculation. If we can tolerate the appearance of some ableist language, it's worth quoting Han at length. The computerlike subject he depicts

> calculates more quickly than the human brain and takes on inordinate quantities of data without difficulty because it is free of all Otherness. It is a machine of positivity [*Positivmaschine*]. Because of autistic self-referentiality, because negativity is absent, an idiot savant can perform what otherwise only a calculator can do. The general positivization of the world means that both human beings and society are transforming into a*utistic performance-machines*. One might also say that overexcited [*überspannt*] efforts to maximize performance are abolishing negativity

16

> because it slows down the process of acceleration. If man were a
> being of negativity [*Negativitätswesen*], the total positivization of
> the world would prove more than a little dangerous. According to
> Hegel, negativity is precisely what keeps existence [*Dasein*] alive.

This formulation may appear to recall the above claims about the uselessness of poetry and, by extension, the purposeless toil of the poet. And indeed, this kind of zombified existence—a neoliberal race to improve ourselves while also earning bragging rights for just how much busyness we've been able to procure—is evident in the research showcases of conceptual and procedural writing, as Place and Fitterman demonstrate. But it's within the wheelhouse of a more broadly defined poetry to demonstrate the distinction between unending, robotic toil and work that, in providing a multivalent depiction of what that is, might be something more.

One recent collection of ostensibly conventional poetry, Catriona Wright's *Table Manners* (2017), shows us how various conceptions of poetic craft can draw attention to just this dynamic. As I've discussed elsewhere, Wright's book takes as its subject the competitive consumption at the heart of what is sometimes called foodie culture. Its treatment of this topic is relentless, even exhausting, in no small part due to its chimingly repetitive sonic devices. One poem begins, "Stylist to star fruit and frozen daiquiris, I understand the right lighting / can detonate salivary glands, expose latent cravings // for mama's ribs or depraved carb binges"; even workplaces depicted as outside the work of socializing and consuming are rendered, for example, as locations that may "suffocate or inspire" the advocacy of oneself as consumer and tastemaker. The collection registers the dynamic of blurred social and professional interactions in service of establishing one's curatorial profile while also presenting a flattened reality in which even a residual compartmentalization of time is absent.

It's not a coincidence that many of the collection's poems depict alcohol as just one more consumable but also a tool for sustaining the omnipresence of this regime. The opening line of "BBQ", "The grapevine is strangling the basil", evokes not only gossip and botanical foodstuffs but also the vineyard. Other images, like "the smell of lighter fluid" and "All the mint from the balcony bathtub has been juleped", employ homemade methods of intoxication in this dynamic, expanding the work-play universe to include hobbies and horticulture. The imagery delves into stoner-party territory ("Dodging our voices, Frank Zappa cackles about rutabagas"), but the final couplet does something a bit different. We see a cloistered, solitary entity in the lines "The catfish grows oily and succulent in its foil shroud, / cayenne-dusted whiskers igniting the air", but we're also reminded of the online term "catfish", or one who presents oneself as something one is not. It marinates in intoxicants, the sensing apparatus of its whiskers locking in with the batshit electric vibes of Zappa; what it all might show us is the extent to which the barbecue's attendees, for all their supposed quirks, have been conditioned not only by the regime of taste and distinction but by literally botanical and biological renderings, including most especially the intoxicants that seem to sustain Wright's speakers' participation in this economy of prestige. There's a wholeness of self, style, and time here that is much different from the blurring of hours and desires seen in Wayman's poems.

The zaniness of Wright's subject matter and its abundant, almost musical, sonic resonances draw attention to the all-encompassing nature of competitive consumption as well as the limitation inhering in the poems' formal traditionalism—limitations that foreclose the possibility of attaining the hand-head reunification Sennett envisions in liberatory enactments of craft. This is something different from direct political attacks on poetry's limited institutional resources; it's a poetic engagement with work that goes beyond Wayman's supplementary form of poetic labour that fetishizes the so-called real thing, or Purdy's easing into the rhythms of poetry's travails.

Take Wright's "Celebrity Chef": it encapsulates this dynamic by beginning with a ritual of performed peril in which the chef "moves through the world with the confidence / of a matador / who marinates his sword in barbecue sauce". In the second stanza, the lines "In Finland, he eats reindeer steaks and cunt- / shaped pastries", add the quality of being respectful of Indigenous cuisines and traditions while also illustrating the misogynistic masculinity of the adventurer. The penultimate stanza builds on the culinary cliché in which the worldly chef has no fear of boundaries between high and low culture:

> Feijoada. Adobo. Offal links. Sardinas con arroz. Zoodles.
>   He is equally happy berating
>   philistines and plumping dumplings with grandmas.

The practice of rejecting binaries between high and low—would anyone interested in any of the arts today not claim to support or do this?—is posed here as just our default setting, reflected as it is in the omnipresent attitudes of televised popular culture.

The above stanza shows us this sameness in other ways, too. Note the alternating *a* and *z* that happens across "Adobo," "arroz," and "Zoodles." The poem's final lines—

> He loves his cameraman like mint
>   loves lamb. He drinks
>   himself into a dungeon every night and every day
>
> he eats his way out.

—tie all the too-much together, completing the pattern with which every stanza seems to demonstrate some ostensible transcendence of limitations or binaries but actually shows us something like Han's overabundance of positivity. The mutating pronouns (he-himself-he-his) play around with the supposedly individual subject of a lyric poem, parodying their ability to navigate the waves of abundance as they sustain the cyclical, quotidian push of the perpetually half-drunk subject. The enjambment that's so regular in both the most basic free verse and Wright's type of formally nuanced lines is here questioned or delayed by the swaths of white space; the result is that the words "a dungeon every night and day" exist simultaneously on their own and with the sense of the longer sentence construction, the temporal cycle of the alcoholic at once jarringly unnatural and just the way of things, at least in the way we live now.

But the work of poetry is more than just our ability to register our present moment of neoliberal hell. Just as Wright probably wouldn't characterize her work as relevant only for its enactment of the always-on lifestyles characterizing our cultural moment, so poetry as vocation or craft, with its lifelong pointlessness, manages to be something for itself even as they embody our very failure to find political solutions to our situation.

It shows us Han's miserable world of everything happening all the time, and ourselves doing it as hard as we can. But, in doing so using the tools of poetry—whatever tools we've got, but, most importantly, those basic devices and repetitions we think of as old-school—also shows us that we might have the ability to do a little more than might seem to be the case. It's a fitting extension of Purdy's and Wayman's engagements with the nature of work, doubled into example in that the poem itself is work. Wright's verse represents our new kind of work by being so obviously and entertainingly on autopilot, but, more importantly, it shows us the value in seeking something else even as the lines of our poetry might themselves be the cage in which our potential is contained. I think there's more value in that than there is in liquidating it all—its blood and sweat and booze—for the sake of reclaiming what little value there is in the blank pulp of the physical books themselves.

Reviewing Reviewing

Debutantes: Conversations on New Voices in Poetry, subsequently rebranded *Debbie*, a short-lived reviews site for debut collections run by Aaron Boothby and Klara Du Plessis, purports to take as guidance "the playful, the messy, the essay as a record of trying to write about what is unfamiliar because it is new". The "About" page continues,

> We acknowledge the uncertainty of reviewing as an asset, the fluidity of reaching out to meaning, like translation, which might diverge from the original, transforming into a new text in the process.

> While we review poetry of all styles and by all authors, we delight in reviews with an individual voice, that analyze with subtlety and intelligence, and are situated as an independent genre, both celebrating and embodying poetry.

The statement of editorial principles implies that the criticism the editors have in mind is, well, not criticism in the traditional sense in that it is open-ended rather than evaluative. While they don't say so explicitly, the premise implies that a debut collection is somehow more unfamiliar than a new offering by someone whose work or name we might recognize. At the very least, the ambiguity of the phrasing itself implies an enhanced degree of openness to whatever might exist in the text, on its own terms and free from the baggage of comparisons.

But even the most established author had a debut; and any piece of writing, especially one published by a recognized entity, exists in a comprehensible landscape of antecedents. Instead of free-from-expectations beneficence, the above statement might indicate an editorial sleight of hand. The underlying belief that poetry can or ought to exist beyond any confines of comparison is expressed more explicitly by Boothby in an early-2020 piece in the *Town Crier* (part of a series on reviewing). Here, Boothby opens by stating that the term review itself "feels caught up in categorization and analysis, activities I'd rather not participate in". (He goes on to reject practices of "reducing the particular to the documented, placing what's alive *under consideration*", and, in a somewhat qualified way, the existence of "what's called Canadian Literature".) Sanchari Sur, also contributing to the series, states that they review "with intention", choosing books "that I genuinely believe have voices that need to be amplified", elevating the concerns of demographic representation above the practices of evaluating or categorizing (really even comparing) that Boothby denigrates.

Evident here is a trend of rejecting the harshness, or perhaps even violence, of the broadly defined evaluative mode, even in the sense of an academically informed reviewing practice that avoids overly subjective assessments (see, for instance, the otherwise peer-reviewed journal *Canadian Literature*, where forty to sixty pages out of an average of 180 are regularly given over to book reviews). That harmful genre is the same one that Jan Zwicky and Michael Lista argued about in a now well-known pair of pieces published in *The Malahat Review* and the *National Post*, respectively.[1] To paraphrase as briefly as possible, Zwicky took the position that the negative review is harmful and unnecessary, and that we ought to reserve the little space devoted to reviews for positive assessment of what truly moves us and politely ignore what doesn't. Lista's rebuttal in the *Post* ridiculed Zwicky's claims that poets could be literally killed by harsh criticism and that only positive appraisals can be truly attentive to their subject matter; the subsequent back-and-forth didn't move the debate forward except insofar as it became increasingly charged with the rhetoric of identity. The consensus that has followed seems to a) permit minor

---

1   See Zwicky, "The Ethics of the Negative Review", and Lista, "The Good in Bad Reviews".

criticism on the level of form; b) discourage wholly or even mostly negative assessments; and c) absolutely forbid any criticism of an author who is ostensibly more oppressed than the reviewer (that is, no punching down). Shane Neilson has detected a confluence of such rules in "We Shall Know You by Your Reviews: The New White Male and Alden Nowlan's *Collected Poems*", arguing that this new consensus permits a negative review provided that the reviewer take aim at an unoppressed author whose work could be regarded as violating progressive orthodoxies.

Possibly in part a response to this ostensible Zwicky-Lista dichotomy, there's been a recent uptick in what might be characterized as a third way of reviewing—neither boosterism nor snark but instead a postmodernist approach in which a text is excavated on its own terms and, sometimes, explored or extended in a creative style that prides itself on an anti-assessment outlook. Two missions coexist here: aesthetic appreciation and creative documentation of one's experience of a book. As much as possible, marginalized identity groups are amplified. See, for instance, the identity-centric takes alongside Boothby's in the aforementioned *Town Crier* series on book reviewing, as well as the first issue of the recently rebooted *Carousel*, the table of contents of which, as it existed in condensed form on the journal's website, closes with a section called USEREVIEW 001-012. The section is described as *"featuring traditional and experimental book reviews"* and valuing diversity in both reviewers and texts reviewed. In her introductory editorial, Reviews Editor Jade Wallace provides a genealogy of the experimental review genre that includes similar statements and review pieces from *Jacket2* and *Lemon Hound*, ending with two tenets of the genre as *Carousel* understands it: that a review's form be "left to the discretion of the reviewer" (followed by a list of non-review "guises" experimental reviews might take—fiction, poetry, classified ads, etc.) and, in keeping with what used to be called postmodernist reviewing practice, that "the kind of commentary offered by an experimental review on a text" ought to be "unfixed".[2]

---

2   See *Carousel*, no. 44, Fall 2020. It's worth noting that, despite this section's evident allegiance with the third-way reviewing principles outlined above, the second tenet in Wallace's editorial acknowledges that "There are

All of which is to say that, whatever its shortcomings, the field of poetry reviewing in Canada certainly doesn't lack a diversity of opinion. What I haven't seen much of, however, is interrogation of the third, in some quarters possibly ascendant style of postmodern or creative reviewing with which I began this essay. For that reason, I want to look more closely at this reviewing technique, considering first the practice of a figure who is as slippery—indeed, almost as undefined—as he is omnipresent in the world of contemporary Canadian poetry, and whose range of prose writing might yield some insight into what, exactly, this other form of reviewing is and does. The short answer is that it may be less reviewing and more describing or showcasing. The longer answer, which I'll elaborate below, is that I think the capaciousness of the traditional term *review* is still valuable, and that its potential can be better realized by taking cues from a responsibly evaluative criticism that splices scholarship and casual or real-time engagement with a new work of poetry.

Not a Uniquely Canadian Problem
Despite what some readers will probably consider the tiresomeness of the Lista-Zwicky affair, taking a wider view suggests that these problems aren't specific either to poetry or to Canada. "If book reviewing in America has declined", writes Gail Pool in *Faint Praise: The Plight of Book Reviewing in America* (2007), "it is hard to say from what glorious pinnacle it has descended". What follows is a survey of comments on the beleaguered craft ranging from Andrew Greeley's 1987 description of reviews as "self-important, pompous and supercilious" back through a comparison of reviewers with cannibals and a chastisement for their "lavish encomiums"—comments made in *Portico* and *Monthly Anthology* in 1817 and 1805, respectively. Pool comes out in favour of a robust book reviewing culture, explicitly for the practical reasons that its immediacy—its distinction from academic scholarship being that it requires a quick critical take on new books—is part of what makes it vital. And while she makes

---

arguments to be made for reviews that evaluate" and "reviews that explain" alongside those that "explore" or "perform indescribable other kinds of engagement with books".

recommendations for improving the practice, by finding "better ways to reward reviewers", for instance, she ultimately finds value in the unpretentious and yet knowledgeable, fair yet evaluative role a good review plays in public (not just elite) discourse.

Phillipa K. Chong, in *Inside the Critics' Circle: Book Reviewing in Uncertain Times* (2020), focuses on fiction reviews, updating Pool's take on the ongoing value of the discourse—that is, not only its documentation of specific critics' thoughts about specific books, but also its ability to indicate "critics' general beliefs about good books, good literary citizenship, and the proper place of art in contemporary society".[3] Chong gives us a more qualified and dispassionate version of Pool's empowering conclusion, arguing that critics function less as "powerful tastemakers" and more already precarious workers whose reviewing practices tend to cause greater uncertainty about said practices and even "a great deal of vulnerability". While this latter point is true, it also means that the reviewer has a degree of power, or at least maneuverability.

Both Pool and Chong make points that indicate the special position of reviewing in relation to scholarship, more generalist commentary, and just some kind of healthy artistic or intellectual citizenship. Chong's point that "In the case of book reviewer, book reviewing can be described as a *switch-role reward structure*, wherein authors are invited by the editors of book review pages to temporarily *switch* from their roles as *producers of books* to perform the role of *reviewer of books*—and then switch back again" is especially relevant to the Canadian world of poetry reviewing. When it comes to writers reviewing writers, Chong describes publishing a positive review in this ecosystem as "a relatively unproblematic task" in which everyone benefits. When it comes to negative reviews, however, people tend not to take

---

3   Although Chong's book focuses on journalistic reviewers (as opposed to essayistic or academic reviewers), poetry reviewing occasionally merits journalistic reviews in Canada but more often comprises reviews "published in more selective or specialized journals, such as monthly or quarterly literary reviews, and targets readers who have a specific interest in literature and some literary background. Rather than selecting from the entire pool of newly published works, these essayists typically select a small number of titles from those that have already received some attention from journalistic reviewers since this attention in itself conveys something about the quality or value of the novels".

down competing writers but instead to "play nice", the "overall intended effect" of which "is to downplay critics' own negative feelings toward a book and to skew the overall valence of a review in a more positive direction". She identifies both benevolent and "defensive" reasons for playing nice: they didn't want to hurt feelings, but they also sought to avoid reprisals. But she also finds a double standard in that reviewers often felt the need to punch up, not down. Chong's astute observations themselves indicate the uniqueness of the genre as it is practiced—or, ought to be more frequently practiced—in contemporary Canadian poetry. Reviewing, in other words, has the potential to be more quickly and robustly generative than does scholarly criticism proper.

Meanwhile, Back in Canada

While normies might take it for granted that a book review should assess the good and bad points of a work, even someone like me learned very quickly that contemporary poetry has its own, quite different set of social and behavioural norms. The book-reviewing method I found myself employing, first unconsciously and then more deliberately, was to avoid the hatchet job at all costs. If I really hated a book I had to write about, I would shift into a comparatively constructive or generative conversation about a larger topic. Or, as Chong more cynically puts it, "Other ways critics played nice include filling the review with contextual details to crowd out any explicit evaluative statements about the book's overall quality or shifting the focus of the review from the merits of the particular book under review to broader criteria". I found that I could spend a lot of time on those broader criteria, so, when I had to, I did.

What interests me more than these vaguely Victorian (or just upper middle-class?) behavioural enforcements is the discursive binary at the centre of the conflict. Michael Warner, in the essays that make up *Publics and Counterpublics* (2002), has provided many tools to help disassemble these different points of view. The fundamental distinction Warner explores, between journalistic and intellectual discourses, along with the different publics that are summoned by and in turn shape these discourses, is particularly useful in determining just why the slash-and-burn reviews of Carmine Starnino, Jason Guriel, and, in arguably their most extreme form, Lista, provoked such ire in the world of Canadian literary commentary and scholarship, even as their authors insisted that such reviewing was the intellectual and stylistic shot in the arm these very communities needed to survive.

Indeed, referring to "the world of Canadian literary commentary and scholarship", as I've done here, both obscures and reveals the slippage at the centre of the conflict. Warner writes of the "extreme segregation of journalistic and intellectual publics" in the United States, characterizing the milieu of the former as a "world of strangers" who are "either directly certified in advance by institutions and networks or indirectly limited by the distributional practices of the publisher". I could make few improvements in terms of either concision or precision to Warner's writing on this subject, so I'll quote him at length:

> Readers share reference points, career trajectories, and subclass interests. They share protocols of discourse, including things like an axiomatic preference for complexity. ("Actually, I believe it's more complicated than that" is, within the academic world, an unanswerable shibboleth; it articulated a professional mode for producing more discourse and for giving it an archivally cumulative character. The same gesture falls hopelessly flat in journalistic settings, where the extensive uptake of audience attention is at a premium.) Writers in this world are inevitably involved in a different language game from journalists.

The contributions of the journalist or pundit accordingly engage in a form of public address in which uptake and reference occur "not in closely argued essays but in an informal, intertextual, and multigeneric field" in which the classical intellectual's attention to complexity carries considerably less weight.[4]

While the world of Canadian poetry criticism could at this point not reasonably be called multigeneric, the format of the book review is, as Pool and Chong have recognized, a hybrid or

---

4   Indeed, Warner's description of this containment of expertise—"There is no reason why intellectuals should be specially positioned for public address in this sense, except where they are packaged as experts"—is almost haunting when read in our historical moment of meta-punditry.

compromise mode that draws from literary scholarship (read: academic writing) as well as the journalistic prose Warner characterizes as fundamentally at odds with the professionalized public of literary scholarship proper.

One strength of the combative reviews of Starnino, Lista, and Guriel is their participation in the journalistic sphere. And Starnino, perhaps the figurehead of this brand of poetry criticism, is anything but unsophisticated in his approach to poetry and his wide-ranging knowledge of and opinions about the form and its history in Canada. At the same time (as will be discussed in greater detail later), moving beyond his often bang-on local readings and into the moments at which he articulates a greater poetics reveals that his brand of criticism exists apart from literary scholarship as it would likely be defined by those in the academy. His reliance on subjective notions of force and effectiveness, despite being couched in his insistence that true innovation involves incrementally adding to tradition, persist in reifying ideas of universally recognizable craft. Despite Starnino's knowledge and idiosyncrasies, his is, it must be said, an arch-conservative view of poetics in terms of preservation and incrementalist modification. In Warner's terms, he's working subjectively and making contributions that are meant to provoke in the moment; he's something like a well-meaning pundit who can be packaged as an expert when the discourse demands it.

Starnino's work is thus ripe to be taken apart in the sphere of academic literary criticism. For the literary critic, doing so can seem like shooting fish in a barrel given Starnino's at times open scorn of the idea that issues of demographic representation (like when, in an infamous interview with *Contemporary Verse 2*, he referred dismissively to Canadian Women in the Literary Arts' "annual 'count'" of women's literary contributions and the "panicky responses around it") are as vital to literary commentary as are truly critical engagements with aesthetics. But it would be incorrect, not to mention insulting to Starnino, to state that his reviews disregard scholarly precedents or mores entirely.

Perhaps this is why his reviews have been attacked not just by casual commentators but also by writers whose creative practice is bound up with the sensibilities of the academy. Lynn Crosbie, for example, referred to him in a piece in *University of Toronto Quarterly* as "the fractious attack budgie of Canadian poetry", his poetry as "weak and gutless", and his anthology as beset by "squawking, preening, and puke". All this in a piece that also claimed the reviewer would not point out the weaker entries in the anthology because she did not "wish to carve a tiny niche for myself by attacking other writers"—suggesting again that criticism-as-journalistic-salvo might not be as separate from the more dignified scholarly discourses as some suspect!

But there have also been more decorous engagements with Starnino's work, including not only reviews but the odd scholarly piece. As early as 2009, Katye Seip's "Exile and Audience: Carmine Starnino and the Poetics of Engagement" appeared in *Canadian Poetry* (a journal of literary scholarship if there ever was one); the article engages in good faith with Starnino's work, suggesting his record as a book reviewer in a sense works in tandem with his poetry's use of direct address, which, along with other techniques of reader engagement, produces a "non-regional, perhaps internationally accessible poetry". I suspect that Starnino wouldn't find either the thoughtful engagements or the takedowns as particularly insulting. His adeptness, and his uniqueness, lies in that he fulfills both roles—being a pundit, inciting an audience, and benefiting from increased engagement with the topic while also leaving a record of informed, if often subjective and less often truly inflammatory, critical work for the depersonalized academic record. But expounding on the utility and shortcomings of Starnino et al. is nothing new, just as decrying the all-positive review as shallow ad copy likely won't provide us with new insights into reviewing as a genre. Perhaps that third genre of purportedly distanced, objective, creative reviewing might, however, by either positive or negative example, show us a better way?

Post-Reviewingism

rob mclennan, in addition to his prolific output in poetry, prose, and genres in between, regularly posts reviews and related commentary on his network of linked blogs. mclennan's critical practice is also unique in terms of how he engages with a text and how he formats his reviews. Still, his practice seems to be in line with a reviewing ideology that both steers clear of negativity and remains attuned to the supposedly incomparable particularities of a piece of literary writing.

mclennan's tendency in his review-like blog posts is to begin with a solid swath of text, without any introduction or anticipatory commentary, and then jump straight into his own critical "take" on the text. See, for example, a recent review that's typical mclennan in format and engagement:

Monday, December 21, 2020
Annick MacAskill, Murmurations

CEREMONIAL
Post-shower my hair still smells of bonfire.
We ate hot dogs bubbled to black char
and watched the rangers chase away the elk,
Her limbs virgules as she fled on the diagonal.
We've been waiting for the birch to bloom.
after vodka in two different bars,
you lead me off the path.
My glasses fog with your breath, our mouths
made visible by the strings of Christmas lights
you hung from the adolescent birch trees—
like the eggs of songbirds, radiant—

the holiday displaced into mid-spring.

Absent even the "review of" that makes the serviceable, MLA-style non-title of the standard book review, mclennan begins with merely the title of MacAskill's collection and a sample of what's inside. Next comes a paragraph that is by turns descriptive (the collection is "[c]onstructed as five sections of short lyrics after an opening poem") and interpretive ("[t]he poems are fueled by tone, texture and language, utilizing narrative structure as a means to an end, as opposed to an end unto itself"). On the level of evaluation, mclennan is enthusiastic—but that should go without saying, given that he's already chosen to devote space to the book. His take cuts itself off somewhat abruptly, however, with the remainder of the post given over to an excerpt from an interview with the author conducted by Alli Vail as part of the

Victoria Festival of Authors, which took place shortly before the date of mclennan's post.[5]

To some extent, mclennan stays true to the postmodern or third-way reviewing technique as I've outlined it above, a similar example being one of Wallace's many contributions to the USEREVIEW column, which begins, "Emily Skov-Nielsen's debut poetry collection, *The Knowing Animals* (Brick Books, 2020), integrates the small, prosaic dramas of mundanity ('I'm bent over the cutting board slicing tomatoes / with a serrated knife — deciding if I should leave you') and luxuriously lyrical imagery ('coltsfoot clambers / from concrete clefts, groundlings of the groundsel tribe, / lovers of rifts and shambles, larvae food for the Gothic moth'), the short piece's three sentences consisting of 117 words, 58 of which belong to Skov-Neilsen's book or refer directly to its publication info. Each piece is a deliberate act of letting the text speak for itself, existing as, respectively, the first thing or most of what we read in the review. To return to mclennan, what follows seems like a combination of the properly "critical" work of interpretation with an open-minded blurbing that is also somewhat commercial (though never crassly so); or, perhaps, an expanded version of the back-cover blurb, other paratext (such as the interview, a link to mclennan's review of MacAskill's previous book), and descriptive notes that exist on a continuum with the comments on backstory, method, and inspiration that are increasingly a standard feature at the end of poetry collections. What's more, the boundary between mclennan's critical work and his work as a publisher is virtually non-existent.[6] His collapsing of these boundaries works well

---

5   See the full post at http://robmclennan.blogspot.com/2020/12/annick-macaskill-murmurations.html/.

6   The singularity of mclennan's outlook is evident given the similarity of the format of his reviews with those of the email updates sent out to the above/ground mailing list, most of which notify subscribers of newly released chapbook titles. There's something to be said for the holistic nature of mclennan's practice, in which a straight-up advertisement shares with his book reviews a humble reluctance to impose interpretation on a work. In both formats, mclennan presents his text as is, displaying its characteristics and providing information that will assist prospective readers in going further with it themselves. It's a consistent, inviting, seemingly genuine invitation for readers to look for whatever kind of meaning or experience they want from the poetry in question.

given his unique position as publisher, author, organizer, and commentator. But is this practice really what we expect from a book review, especially considered in terms of the genre's wider cultural function as discussed by Pool and Chong?

Ultimately, it's not what a lot of people would describe as poetry criticism—it's engaging and has mclennan's stamp on it, but it's exactly what undergraduate students are told not to do— open a paragraph or an entire essay with some epigraph-like slice of the work, as though it speaks for itself and the essay couldn't possibly have anything to add. (So why am I reading the essay?) Next comes lessons about integrating quotations with our work, and with not ending a paragraph with a quotation because an excerpt of an author's work should always be followed by some kind of interpretation or commentary, or illumination, or whatever, that comes from us. mclennan must know all this, of course. The anti-negative-review people, whether they're of Zwicky's stripe or examples of a third way, surely do. The point seems to be that, in their unwillingness to let their own voice step all over a text, they're taking a step back, or aside, from what most readers understand the function of a review to be.[7]

As part of this preference to give readers more of the book itself, we see some other common practices that emerge. mclennan at times seems to heed Chong's advice to shift to "broader criteria" to avoid negativity, frequently doing so by drawing on his familiarity with various local personalities, keen understanding of the genesis of various projects of which he writes, and deep knowledge of the literature of specific cities (such as Ottawa, especially, but also fleeting scenes in Edmonton and elsewhere). Another strategy, similar to that seen in Wallace's USEREVIEW piece but longer and more involved, is visible in Alan Reed's treatment of Anahita Jamali Rad's *For Love and Autonomy* (2016), which appeared in *Debbie*. Reed inhabits and extends the style of the book being reviewed—in the block quotations from the book

---

7   For many in the university, this attitude appears to be part of a trend that is larger, and, at least to my mind, indicative of the creeping values of neoliberalism—that is, a reluctance to "teach to" our students in favour of letting them take the wheel, sharing their unique experiences and whatever other knowledge they already possess.

and short swaths of lucid prose that, like in the collection, at a few points gently defamiliarize subjectivity as it exists in common grammatical constructions ("Who is the lyric poem?"; "what love, what autonomy, what poetry is possible under the conditions of late capitalism?"). Reed also briefly reflects on the book's format—specifically, the fact that the book's sale price is printed on its back above the barcode. But the purpose of the review is to reiterate and make a supplementary argument in support of the author's premise that social and historical determinisms require that we consider "what subject and what speech is possible from within a lyric grounded firmly in the material conditions and 'clumsy ideologies' framing its lived reality, a reality firmly circumscribed by the systemic oppressions of capitalism". Reed creates an odd resonance by repeating the formulation "she/Jamali Rad writes", followed by a quotation from the poems, four times in the short review, echoing the author's style to reinforce her ideas about voice and agency.

This kind of stylistic imitation and reiteration or amplification of a work's premise, approach, or ideology can be interesting in itself, just as additional details about a book object or the personalities and circumstances associated with its germination might be useful. Still, it seems strangely frivolous to foreground these as a reviewing practice in itself. What results could more accurately be described as a showcase than a review; maybe more importantly, the difference between this approach and the boosterism that's arguably inherent to Zwicky's conception of responsible book reviewing isn't quite apparent.

Hybrid Criticisms?

When it comes to the review format, I find part of myself instinctively siding with the difficult critics—the negative reviewers. When done well, there's a meaningfulness to this kind of contribution that isn't always evident in the thoughtfully descriptive or self-consciously artistic third option. At the same time, inciting an audience and getting attention, Warner's journalism-sphere descriptors, don't do justice to the ability of the provocative review to generate more (ideally) incisive commentary—commentary that can leave behind for scholars a record of informed critical work in its early stages or, potentially, a forum of debate vigorous enough to punch holes into areas where either studied scholarship or the methodical, careful respectfulness of the third way might not venture. But this documentation of the early work into reading and situated poems is, in spite of the ad hoc nature of the moment, not entirely separate from the established discourses of academic literary criticism. Du Plessis, for instance, has written of a "weird ageism" in the practice of Canadian poetry reviewing:

> Not considering the lag of a year or even two after a book's release before the publication of some reviews, reviews favour the newcomers to the scene. Every spring and fall herald a whole new cohort of books, and once an author has moved from the release of one book to their next, chances for a review of the earlier book are very slim. People don't review books that were released five, ten, twenty years ago. Instead, reviews mature into essays. As a book's seniority in its social circle increases (and if it is endowed with a glow of luck), it also enters institutional settings—academics present papers about it, books are published about it, students study it and write term projects about it. In other words, young books receive review-essays and older books graduate to essay-essays.

Du Plessis ultimately questions this process, wondering whether reviews could be "rebranded" as essays, thereby revealing instances of the format as "someone's intellectual engagement with literary output, an energizing burst of insights, a sharing, one fragment of a conversation". But isn't this already happening, at least in the responsibly evaluative review? Perhaps we just don't think about it, or don't want to think about it for as long as we're busy denigrating a more narrowly defined method of reviewing. Like the combative questioning of an identity-hidden reviewer taking on a scholarly piece, they are (in most cases, one assumes) occupying this position for the sake of vetting the article and ensuring the quality of what is allowed to enter the discourse. The momentary, situational unpleasantness means that the larger system is working. The oversights or even mistakes of the most casual contemporary review show us the parts moving at the lowest levels.

That's why an informed practice of evaluative criticism— one that is nevertheless cognizant of the generic hybridity of the form—is so necessary. That's the work I already see being done in the reviews I get the most from, percolating beneath the surface of the review even as it functions conventionally. That's why I'll finish with an equally reviled and respected writer of both reviews and scholarly works. In the preface to Marjorie Perloff's recent two-volume selected book reviews, *Circling the Canon* (2019), editor David Jonathan Bayot considers a passage from a keynote address Perloff delivered at an event organized by the Poetry Center in Wuhan, China.[8] Here Perloff describes: writing an omnibus review in 1973; in turn being led to look closely at a 1970 anthology, Ron Padgett and David Shapiro's *An Anthology of New York Poets*; deciding to focus in the review on Frank O'Hara, one of the contributors to the anthology; finding a copy of O'Hara's *Art Chronicles* the next year at the Museum of Modern Art; deciding to review the book in *The New Republic*; and the review coming to the attention of a publisher who gave her a contract to write her landmark *Frank O'Hara: A Poet Among Painters* (1977). Bayot marvels at the way a "(dis) interested review" had exposed Perloff and her readers to "a brave new world of poetry or, more precisely, a different and differential way of knowing and engaging with 'poetry' as, first of all, a practice in context, that is, a 'language game'".

The story shows how reviewing is interwoven with opportunities, larger projects, and, in this case, one's mode of scholarly engagement. I don't think this is a one-off scenario, or one specific to the younger Perloff's era or milieu. In fact, I'm increasingly convinced that reviewing is today where the critical action happens, with the genre's haphazard hypotheses subject to the "peer review" of a less specialized but more real-world, combative space of an increasingly online, real-time forum for discussion and critique. However crass, this forum is at the forefront of literary debate or engagement in the same way that the review might function as the earliest approximation of literary-critical interpretation. (It's also free from the

---

8   The address was published as "Becoming a Critic: An Academic Memoir" in *Epsians* 2 (2012): 1-24 and reprinted in Perloff's *Poetics in a New Key: Interviews and Essays*, edited by David Jonathan Y. Bayot, U of Chicago P, 2013, pp. 3-27.

interminable, seemingly worsening delays that characterize academic publishing.)

Even aside from the practicalities of this system, the review retains a certain aura. Perloff, no stranger to controversy in any of her critical writing, nevertheless uses the review to really go places. There are several moments scattered throughout *Circling the Canon* in which Perloff simply *demands more* than what a book is giving her. She laments in a 1984 review of various translations of French poetry that, in the US literary climate at the time, "even French is coming to be regarded as the Exotic Other" and that, as a result, "we are beginning to see a number of collaborative translations in which an American poet works with a French scholar". "We have long accepted this situation", Perloff continues, "when it comes to, say, Arabic or Hungarian (although even in the case of these languages, one wonders what it means to have A. furnish literal glosses that B. then renders 'poetic')" ("The French Connection"). Perloff's disapproval of this arrangement will be bad news for virtually any American "translator" of Chinese poetry. But why stop there? Years later, in a 2001 review of William Gass' *Reading Rilke: Reflections on the Problems of Translation* (2000), she again questions "the curious premise that the poet-translator (usually male) takes the trot generated by his informant (usually, in the current economy, female) and endows those words with something called 'poetry'" ("Reading Gass Reading Rilke"). Several pages after noting that "James Joyce, let's recall, taught himself Norwegian just so that he could read Ibsen", she recounts another indication of our lack of poetic and scholarly ambition:

> At a recent poetry festival where she was asked about her influences, a highly respected American poet spoke movingly about her special attachment to Rilke. Afterward, I asked her if she could read Rilke in German. She said no. I then asked her what translation she was using. She couldn't quite remember. "Have you ever wanted to take time off to learn a little German so that you might have a sense of Rilke's sound and rhythm?" I asked. She merely shrugged, as if to say that such study would be too much of a chore for a successful mid-career poet like herself.

Perloff explicitly refers to the ambition of the mid-career poet, but she could equally be discussing the sterile, professionalized practice of the literary critic—or, in Canada (it must be said), almost anybody who winds up publishing poetry reviews. Perloff's criticism is made on the first line of critical engagement (here a review of another attempt to render the work of a frequently translated author). And it's made in a review, itself neither couched in one of Perloff's monographs, nor collected alongside her scholarly articles, but included in a late-career, two-volume miscellany of nothing but her reviews! The genre is more easily produced than a scholarly monograph, of course, but it's because of that very haphazard nature that the review has a swagger—a sense of possibility but also expectation. A responsible book-length engagement with a particular method of translation will almost invariably treat that method on its own terms, granting it the legitimacy required for this kind of critical engagement to exist at all. The humble format of the review pays no such respects. And while this means that a bad reviewer can be careless, or unreasonable, or a nagging irritation, a reviewer with Perloff's knowledge and insight has every right to demand more of its object. Paradoxically or not, the unassuming, quasi-scholarly form of the review is often where the action is.

Referring to this vitality seems at odds with the very real considerations that unfortunately, and for some reason especially in this country, colour any responsible reviewing practice. Even I, for instance, worry as much about demographics, reputation, and, still more selfishly, my own record of writing and semi-scholarly (readerly?) engagement whenever I pitch reviews or select titles from booklists. I wonder if the constellation of the benefits of reviewing that I've outlined here would be better served by a truly phenomenological approach to reviewing: doing so with an eye to the churning economy that produces what is reviewed. What if someone just reviewed three, or five, or twenty new books of poetry every year, but they didn't have a choice as to which ones? Conversely, what if someone reviewed that many books that were entirely of their choosing, independent of any pragmatic or professional concerns? Although I suspect the latter possibility might be mutually exclusive with pretty much any notion of literary or reviewing expertise, I'm still tempted to think that the track record of either hypothetical reviewer would be more interesting than what we get from the standard review collection.

As Pool acknowledges, complaints about the practice will persist. Obviously there's corruption—these aren't disinterested agents as much as the reader-writers of poetry, who will reliably help their friends and denigrate their enemies. Then again, the title of this essay is equal parts lament and imperative. Chong understands the practice of reviewing as something to be studied; as an area in which commentary and commentary about commentary is now the subject not of amateur punditry but scholarship itself. As Chong's conclusion characterizes the problem, "[w]hat it means to be a writer is unclear, as the boundaries of that category can be quite blurry as well. For many, seeing one's name signed on a review served as an objective signal of one's belonging to the wider literary community". It's a simple signal, and one that doesn't count for much in terms of personal gains. But it's also the fabric that holds together those bigger achievements, buoying or sinking them, flowing into the spaces separating university departments from open mics from (un)original geniuses and, by definition, connecting them. I'm fine with calling that kind of writing whatever name we know it by.

I Just Wrote This Five Minutes Ago: Expectations, Originality, and the Contemporary North American Poetry Reading

The weirdness of the contemporary North American poetry reading has been discussed before. But it seems like there's always some newly disorienting example of preposterousness waiting in the wings—something poetry's practitioners have seen a hundred times but, because of our proximity, haven't been able to notice until some bewildered observation from a non-poet brings it into view. I'm not talking about the affected and artificial "poet voice", which is regularly denigrated. I'm talking about small behaviours other than the act of the poet's reading: how they introduce themselves or their work, or even the degree of seriousness their mannerisms suggest they're bringing to the endeavour. Perhaps the ultimate litmus test for the poetry reading involves bringing an average, gainfully employed twenty- or thirty-something to their first acknowledged-as-such poetry reading. In my experience, nearly all such figures balk at an entirely alien form of stupidity that the rest of us for some reason gladly, or at least voluntarily, endure.

Poet voice and other frustrations with the format are categorizable, in terms of what they tell us about the role of performance in contemporary poetry and in terms of the larger constellation of practices I'm trying to investigate. Scholarly interrogations of poet voice, for example, have found that the zany poet figure works hand in hand with continuing valorization of the written word. Lesley Wheeler, for instance, gives an account of the evolution of poetic voice from professional performance to the unprofessional presence of the poet herself, while Brian Reed provides an especially comical takedown of the entire smalltime extravaganza of

> the poet who writes well by any conventional measure but who also gives poetry readings that resemble excruciatingly bad, low-tech theater. How much longer, one often wonders, will audiences endure paper-shuffling, mic-incompetence, hem-haw-choked prefatory anecdotes, and clichéd deliveries that range from breathless poète to profound orotundity to randomly synCOpaTED Beatnickery? Readings of this ilk perpetuate the old modernist trope that the written page is the repository of true value and that oral performance degrades or distracts from the contemplation of verse's deeper significance.

It's all funny—as funny as the behavioural and non-verbal quirks I'll run through here. But I do so for a different reason: to identify the unspoken expectations that lie behind the frustrations. These expectations reveal that there is an enduring preoccupation with text-based notions of originality and craft, as Wheeler and Reed have pointed out. They also indicate an affirmative element behind the weirdnesses of contemporary poetry: that is, the ability of the latter to create a space for a work that is meaningful precisely because its oddness ensures it remains undisciplined, unsystematized, and ultimately compassionate.

When I lived in Kingston during my PhD studies, I discovered—late in the game, as usual—local poet and organizer Bruce Kauffman's monthly poetry open mics. I did so at a time when I was exhausted with my program and willing to try new social outings until I was finished with my dissertation. Shortly after attending for the first time, I mentioned the experience to another poetry friend in the area. "So you got to see some crying and some feelings", he quipped. And it's true that there was a lot of the latter, if substantially less of the former. Although there were a lot of young people making up the attendees, the regulars consisted of an older crowd who returned, week after week, reliably intoning the same few chestnuts from their tattered notebooks. I made a few new friends and acquaintances there, one of whom would throw me eyerolls as regulars took the stage. Kauffman's open mics were great in some ways—for community building, for getting people out and trying something new—but in terms of just sitting there and listening to it, it was often pretty bad. I hasten to add here that the dynamic I describe had nothing to do with any particular person in attendance, or with Kingston, or with the open-mic format. The more I think about it, this wonderful, awkward, often shabby ensemble was emblematic of the enduring quirks of the North American poetry reading itself.

Shortly after my time with this community ended, I came across a Twitter prompt by Toronto poet Kathryn Mockler. She asked on July 8th, 2019, "What are some terrible, funny, awkward things poets do at readings? Like read too long, brag too much, etc". Maybe I missed the feelings, or the eyerolls, because I took way too much interest in reading, and then categorizing, the replies. I was especially interested in three of the most commonly held complaints: first, and spurring the title of this book, declarations that poets were reading work written five minutes beforehand; second, that they would spend time reciting other poets' poems; third, readers spending what was perceived as too long a time explaining the poem—sometimes simply its writerly genesis or set of references, and sometimes a more rigorous process (selection, algorithm, writing-through, etc.—conceptualist techniques that have by now found their way into the poetic mainstream).

The first complaint blossomed when Nisa Malli replied, "'I wrote this poem in the cab over / just this morning'. Many others echoed this grievance, bemoaning the poem that was written ten, or five minutes ago, or, more vaguely and still less promisingly, "like, just, right now". Several posters agreed: "That 'I wrote this on the way over' thing! Argh"—as one user, Marion Agnew, put it—"If you imagine your raw thoughts to be so fascinating, well OK, but don't say so". There seemed to be a consensus that this practice implied arrogance and a lack of respect for other people's time and attention. Perhaps the complaint suggests that people expect a bigger variety of readers, or just that they want to get through what they don't like as quickly as possible. Regardless, the complaint's relatability indicates that, even at a low-stakes event like an open mic, the time of the audience, participants, and organizers was worth slightly more than this level of self-indulgence seemed to assume.

Related to this is the second grievance, about the practice of prefacing or interspersing one's own poems with those by other authors. Not authors who are present at the time; not contemporary poets with whom the reader has been collaborating; but well-known authors—usually dead, more usually canonical (at least for the poetry community in question—in my own experience, this phenomenon most frequently features famed Canadian everyman Al Purdy). There was consensus here, too, most eloquently captured in a comment by scholar and writer Jeremy Colangelo, who replied, "Shows up at an open mic with *Howl and Other Poems* in their pocket: 'Alright [before] I get to my own stuff, just to mix things up...'".

The prevalence of complaint number one—that a reader had written their work in five (or whatever) minutes—implies that there is an expectation of work put in in advance. What many of us do *not* want, in other words, is improv. (At least not in the context of the mainstream or middlebrow poetry reading.) Complaint number two—that a reader spends undue time reading the work of those with whom their own writing bears no meaningful relation—implies an expectation of originality, or that the work will be the reader's own (wholly or, sometimes, collaboratively).

Both these complaints suggest that the notion of an authentic voice, as unpacked by Wheeler and others, lives on in that we expect realness to flow from the well-wrought, text-based works that provide the basis for performance. But a third complaint, about long explanatory sections, suggests a different dynamic—one that supersedes the preoccupations with originality and craft that I'll address in a subsequent essay. Namely, several responders lamented "[c]ondescending explanations of references or allusions" in the work, "[o]ver-long" intros "about the origins of the pieces they're reading" (@hebemachia), or even just "those who talk too much between poems" (@robmclennanblog). It may be useful to turn here to Thomas Hodd's *#NoMoreNotes*, a 2016 manifesto against the proliferation of explanatory notes in contemporary poetry collections. After stating that "In each case the majority of the notes are mildly interesting or entertaining at best", Hodd continues:

> According to the poets I consulted, the Notes section allowed them to acknowledge sources they consulted for their 'research.' Yet the notion that poets need to categorize their explorations, life experiences and choices for reading material as 'research' seems to me the product of having written too many grant proposals for an increasingly business-minded cultural industry.

Hodd here complains of the institutionally located nature of contemporary poetry, but he also takes issue with the idea that "poets feel additional information helps the reader to understand the poem better", claiming that other art forms neither employ nor require such explanations.

Hodd's objections resonate with those of the tweeters, who just want the thing itself. No background, no explanation of genesis or method, not even any extra-poetic paratext—just the good stuff. These beefs challenge my thesis: wouldn't the notes suggest that they *did* put the effort in, that they *were* giving us hard work and originality, and simply illustrating as much from angles other than the (page- or performance-centric) final product? If so, a complaint like Hodd's indicates that what people want in such environments would be originality but not any demonstration of process. That is, they want the kind of work that's recognizable solely in the form of a final product, not in the blueprints behind that product. The balance, perhaps, lies in poetry's seemingly being easy enough to have a reasonably finished text ready for presentation—giving listeners, in a publicly oriented or open-mic style event especially, the idea that it's possible for them to participate as well, provided they've made it through the initiation of seeing and hearing how (or just that) it's done and into something that might be called working together. There's a long history in the formations and subcultures that make up Canadian poetry of this tendency to at once privilege poetry's print-oriented products and take as self-evident their status as improvable and thus expendable—ranging at least from Al Purdy and through to more recent, more popular poets I'll look at in the final essay of this section. The issue raised being that perhaps this is a notably, though of course not exclusively, Canadian characteristic, and that this print dynamic is at the centre of that humblest of community poetry events.

And, indeed, ideas of accessibility came up too—another Toronto poet and onetime reading series organizer, Jacob McArthur Mooney, snarkily replied to the thread, "Every time someone reads something they wrote that day I want to ask for my zero dollars back". The tweet seemed to me to have been made in bad faith—obviously we don't measure these things in dollar value alone.[1] But it got me thinking about what value we were really talking about. Maybe what's valuable in the open mic poetry reading is an openness that ensures poetry remains accessible to anyone who wants to engage with the embattled form's paradoxically coexisting uselessness and potentiality. If there is a craft at work in open mics at the level of process, it is this egalitarian ideal that allows people—yes, any people—to ventilate their sometimes just-composed verse.

Some miss that point, though. For those participating in Mockler's thread, the mainstream Canadian poetry reading seems to be based on an expectation that the poet will showcase her craft—that is, display "work" that has already been done and that exists on a primarily textual level; work that is meant for presentation as a reasonably conceived whole the processual nature of which must not be foregrounded.[2] Existing in conjunction with this distrust of the unfinished or in-process state of such works is the complaint about notes, which imply *too much* work or too much systematization. Which may mean that, while the reading, as Peter Middleton has pointed out, plays an intersubjective, mediating role, with the presence of the poet "adding authority" to the uncertain and "enormously complex transactions of institutional legitimation in the contemporary world", it may also be an affirmative or interpellative one,

---

1   One distinction not made by Mockler's complaint prompt was that between scheduled readings and the poetry open mic. Such a distinction was unnecessary given the common gripes, but it matters if we consider questions of value like that raised by Mooney.

2   This despite the fact that, from a scholarly perspective at least, it's common knowledge that the public presentation of even the most lyric of poems is an important step in its compositional evolution.

initiating its listeners into a universe where they too can put work into a poem and present it as a real thing. At least, as long as one undergoes a certain apprenticeship (i.e. taking more than five minutes on a poem). And—don't worry—you don't need to be too rigorous or systematic about it either. Assuming that everyone gets it just right, and tightens the screws just a little more, we can live in a world of poetry readings that don't inspire all those gripes. A perfect world of poetry!

***

To be sure, those gripes are warranted, just on a casual, social level, given some of the cringeworthy stuff that happens at these events. The ever-expanding discourse around poet voice itself suggests that even those most invested in contemporary poetry frequently have a terrible experience at the contemporary reading. But isn't this because contemporary poetry is, as part of its core dynamic, clearing the space to allow that kind of terrible to exist? Raising the question of whether there's something to be admired in that naked, stupid expressiveness? My instinct is to say no, that's not it. But, the more I think about it, what kind of alternative would I prefer? One in which I had stuck around longer in Kingston, taken charge, given some lessons about what I think (and what these pages might at some points be arguing) good poetry is, and reshaped x reading series or y open-mic event so as to cut off the fat? One in which things were really tightened up, so that what we had was a smaller, more discerning crowd, nodding along with each other's new edits each month?

Obviously, and thankfully, the prospect is absurd. Such events sound markedly worse than anything I endured in Kingston. From the distance of a few years, I think there's probably not been a better distillation of everything I find vital in contemporary poetry than I found at those monthly events. As much as I cringed while listening to awful poems, and as much of an irritable bastard I am in general, I don't ever want a publicly accessible poetry world that imposes on its participants restrictions serious enough to mean that they wouldn't have a space to share their work. A space to which they could return in subsequent months—maybe with poems that those more discerning members of the group would deem better, or maybe just with more of the same.

I encountered a similar sentiment among even the stentorian addresses collected in *Measures of Astonishment*, the volume that includes the League of Canadian Poets' annual Anne Szumigalski Lectures. Mark Abley's 2007 address describes a recognizable figure, and a relatable feeling of openness, at work in Szumigalski's informal poetry workshop in Saskatoon in the early 1970s. Abley writes of "an old farmer, Alf Bye, who used to drive up with his wife from the Swift Current area, a good three hours southwest of the city, just to attend the workshop meetings". Abley describes his poetry as "the old-fashioned sort that most of us quietly sneered at—or even, I regret to say, not so quietly sneered at. He wrote about the prairies in sonorous rhyming couplets and florid blank verse that Tennyson would have considered old-fashioned". Remove the prairies from the equation and I recall precisely the same figure—at least one— from those open mics in Kingston.

Abley concludes that, while he thought Alf embarrassing at the time, he could at the distance of decades

> begin to appreciate the man. He loved the English language, he needed to express his emotions, and he took genuine pride in the outmoded verse he produced. Why else would he have driven for hours to sit through meetings where he and his speechless wife must have felt terribly out of place? He had no understanding of modern literature—for him, T.S. Eliot was dangerously radical. But he loved poetry. Anne Szumigalski never made fun of the man. The rest of us were happy when he stopped coming to the meetings, but I'm not sure if Anne shared our relief. She understood both his isolation and his passion for language.

I guess I also went through hating and then gradually understanding the passion—the passion that includes within itself an isolation in focusing on that thing that does nothing, even as all around us it's obscured or cynically commandeered to some other purpose. Maybe that movement, around and through and potentially beyond, is the thing itself.

Minimal Requirements

In a progressive arts culture that seems to scorn the validity of majority opinion and ideas of any mainstream at all, what value is there in describing anything as minor? Aren't we all minor? Or, at least, isn't there a tendency to position ourselves that way? If any of us are really that major, aren't we also supposed to be devoting a good deal of our time to amplifying, researching, or searching for definitively minor aspects of our subculture? Even aside from status and reputation, poetry itself seems to be inherently oriented toward the detailed and the close-up—whether it's imagism or a more-minimal-than-prose take on bigger issues, attention to nuance seems to be a defining feature. Whatever aspect of poetry or poetry culture one chooses to listen in on, minor seems to be the key.

At the same time, however, there's an interesting subset of contemporary poetry that insists on zooming in on the most minor details, devoting itself to the tiniest aspects of an always already smaller literary form. I want to run through a pretty much random sampling of books I've come across, all of which thematize tininess, foreground minute physical details of the craft of poetry publishing, and in the process register the ad-hoc environment of their material and poetic production. They're minor not as in self-defeated, but in that they together help to demarcate a small area of poetic practice, in so doing magnifying and foregrounding itself and its attendant vicissitudes, incongruities, half-knowledges, and self-consciously lower standards and expectations. As such, the kind of minor works I'll look at shortly—by Aaron Giovannone, Cameron Anstee, Souvankham Thammavongsa, Ally Fleming, and Michael E. Casteels—in dealing in the minute, particular, or elementary, function as a compendium of the aesthetics, attitudes, and practices of which they're comprised. They're examples of an aesthetic and material tininess that, counterintuitively, give a glimpse of the non-systematized abundance and variety of their poetic moment.

First, though, it's worth noting that the grains and pulp of this kind of poetry are visible in an old introduction I recently came across—George Bowering's short essay in his *The Contemporary Canadian Poem Anthology* (1983), an interesting account of both coming into poetry and Canadian poetry coming into its own circa the early 1960s to the early 1980s. Bowering begins with the physical act of opening a book, going on to describe "how nice it was in grade one when the teacher would hold a bunch of big oblong cards & turn them to face the class, one by one". The image of the flipping cards continues with those students who "would settle for Business Administration or car theft" forgetting "how wonderful that flipped word could be" and then others dropping out after "flipping a few magazine poems, or maybe a book of poems".

Readings of the physicality of the book-object are today not particularly innovative. Still striking about Bowering's piece, however, is that its images of childhood and school point to the educative element that inheres in poetry's supposedly undisciplined or rough-hewn characteristics, as well as to its expansive or welcoming nature. (The latter characteristic is evident also in the fact that attention to the tangible text is a practice that has crept into larger presses—trade publications and established chapbook presses, including those that, despite their small-press status, would be described by few as meaningfully underground or experimental.) The paper fetish seems also to be more of a thematization of smallness, perhaps a symptom of poetry's accommodation and adoption of formerly underground, smallest-of-small-press practices: a funhouse mirror stood up somewhere inside the literary marketplace. I think poetry that focuses on the textual, the tiny, and the details also, as I'll argue here, responds to poetry's paradoxical centring of itself in the minor by creating the illusion of immensity and fashioning brevity from the excess. Along the way, it recreates the journey-in-miniature Bowering describes, functioning as a succinct record of the cultural practices that make up contemporary poetry's positive work.

Gilles Deleuze and Félix Guattari's "What Is a Minor Literature?" defines the concept as those literatures created by minorities within major languages, meaning that everything in such traditions is politically charged. More specifically, everything in these literatures "takes on a collective value": "Indeed, precisely because talent isn't abundant in a minor literature, there are no possibilities for an individuated enunciation that would belong to this or that 'master' and that could be separated from a collective enunciation". As usual, Deleuze and Guattari have got their own thing going on, but this idea of a minority coming into its own within some larger entity (such as a nation-state, to follow their social and political approach) includes within it both the idea of learning, or initiation into, something larger. The ideal contains a fixation on becomingness, on not yet having been reached. Compared to fiction and nonfiction, it seems like this is pretty much where poetry is at. Of course these comparisons are somewhat arbitrary, but those familiar with contemporary Canadian poetry might indeed find relevant the authors' fixation on a "scarcity of talent", not to mention their statement that what individual authors working in such a tradition contribute, at least in their view, "already constitutes a common action, and what he or she says or does is necessarily political, even if others aren't in agreement".

So is poetry just a perpetually junior partner? It's worth noting a strange passage in the essay that attempts a kind of cross-section of the possibilities of the minor. In it, the authors give us a series of situations we might compare with contemporary Canadian poetry, albeit using the kitschy space-age imagery and terminology that form the Deleuze-Guattari universe:

> There are even more serious examples that cross over between groups. The revival of regionalisms, with a reterritorialization through dialect or patois, a vernacular language—how does that serve a worldwide or transnational technocracy? How can that

contribute to revolutionary movements, since they are also filled with archaisms that they are trying to impart a contemporary sense to? From Servan-Schreiber to the Breton bard to the Canadian singer. And that's not really how the borders divide up, since the Canadian singer can also bring about the most reactionary, the most Oedipal of reterritorializations, oh mamma, oh my native land, my cabin, olé, olé. We would call this a blur, a mixed-up history, a political situation, but linguists don't know about this, don't want to know about this, since, as linguists, they are 'apolitical,' pure scientists. Even Chomsky compensated for his scientific apoliticism only by his courageous struggle against the war in Vietnam.

The essay first appeared in 1986, and it was written from a European perspective. On the one hand, we might puzzle over the strange figure and picture. What kind of Canadian? What kind of song? How funny is it that the authors on the previous page criticize "the indignation of integrationists who cry when Mass is said in French", then refer to classicists bemoaning the decline of Latin as "even more behind the times", only to give us this picture of a native olé?

On the other, the series of considerations takes the shape of mixed-up silliness: it includes anachronism, dysphoria, incorrectness, and, as perhaps a necessary part of this constellation, a possibility for the reactionary. The incongruity of the image makes it that much more accurate a descriptor of whatever it is that's minor about poetry and contemporary poetry especially. The entire constellation of minor and regional and formally ill-defined, messily non-hierarchical stuff (I'm thinking now of the overcited Body without Organs, ironically a centrepiece of Deleuze-and-Guattari lore) that used to be called Poetic Language is a variegated performance of precisely these different things. The essay's attempt at systemizing the minor is as sloppy as the scrappy, idiosyncratic stuff that comprises its subject.

Picking up the thread of the Canadian singer, we might also remember that Canadian poetry—with its smaller numbers and remoteness—is an especially ugly, laughable-when-looking-in-from-the-outside form. But the indeterminacy that inheres in this site of production, with all its random aesthetics, life experiences, and feelings and half-knowing, makes up an invocation not of any politically definable value, or even a clear idea, but instead the nebulous life-stuff of work that is generative and expansive. There's nothing notably Canadian about it, except that the process plays out in a specific cross-section of the kind of multivalently productive poetic work I'm describing. Deleuze and Guattari's politicized conception of minor literatures, dissolving as it does into a tangled, anachronistic mass of unstable oppositions and what, from a Canadian perspective, seem like misconceptions or quirks, seems useful to me in precisely this sense. More than a coincidental resonance, however, the weirdness of their example of looking in from the outside, along with its dated quality, reflects the usefulness of poetry as record of these non-systematic instances of practice, knowledge, and value. Such attention to the minimalism in and the minimal requirements associated with these publication practices—the cranking out of words themselves in some form that documents and can be experienced, despite and because of the low production quality and low stakes—shows a poetry of the multiply minor, a form rendering itself as a laconic, lapidary record of longer poetic discourses and larger cultural practices. But, in the process, this kind of sampling of recent minimal poetry transcends the politicized major-minor distinctions at the centre of Deleuze and Guattari's essay, even if it does so by giving us a tactile, no-stakes document of what's actually there. The books here aren't especially unified in terms of subject matter or politics, or community, or whatever. But highlighting some work that operates in this vein is an interesting exercise in that it sloughs off the burden of expecting a category, or scene, or whatever to signify the politicized or cultural commitments of any conventionally defined school or movement.

Emblematic of this paradox is Thammavongsa, whose attention to the tiny has culminated in a 2020 Giller Prize (for her collection of short stories, *How to Pronounce Knife*). Parts of that book draw on her experiences growing up in a family of Lao refugees, subject matter that has also appeared in far less robustly narrated forms in Thammavongsa's poetry. Her first book, *Small Arguments* (2003), stays small, the tininess of its poems combining with typographical oddities (with many poems printed across the bottom of the book's pages) to make readers feel like they are holding something at once miniature and unwieldy.

The first poem, "Materials", is simplistic even as it is grounded in the textual:

Growing up, I
did not have books

The only reading material
there was

were old newspapers laid out
on the floor

Note the way "was // were" uses solecism as a hinge, providing a shift in perspective as if a camera were zooming in and then panning to take a look from a different angle.

Next is a poem called "The Weight of Salt", then "Water"; then, beginning with "A Pear, Sliced", come poems for fruits, as if the sequence starts with bare minerals and then creates its own world in miniature, a process that continues with "Poem for Trees", "Poem for the Rain", and "The Snow". Beginning the first two titles with "Poem for" seems to put the text at a further remove, creating less immediacy and letting us look carefully, as if anew, at the landscape and weather features that have been at the centre of trite poetry, Canadian and otherwise, for ages. (Subsequent poems are about various bugs, with the exception of one about "Frogs" and "This Sea Shell".)

"A Firefly" condenses the push and pull among various opposites into a seemingly mundane, unremarkable image. The statement "It is a small argument / lending itself to silence" compresses obvious binaries of argument-silence and light-dark, while "a small argument / the sun will never come to hear" anticipates the sun precisely in not surviving that long. The "Darkness" at the end of the poem "opens its palm / to set free a fire // its body could not put down", thus resisting the same darkness that sets it free. But the moving parts are never quite interrogated—they're just there, like the poem's point-of-light conceit and the way its essence is that of the whole book. The point of fire reduces the everyday dynamism of flame to its most elementary unit—not in any literal or molecular sense, but by representing its smallness with a thing we just understand as minuscule in its mundanity.

The entire dynamic is at once strewn comparatively messily and yet perfectly, something that's encapsulated in "Birds, a Description of Them in the Sky", from a subsequent collection, *Light* (2013). Here it is in its entirety:

> A cluster fell to the ground in a small heap, tossed out like bits of unused black fabric
>
> They fell slow and in small batches like ash tapped from the end of a burning cigarette
>
> Any sudden move made a handful leap back, back into that blue upturned tray, that dump, that ash-receiver

Minimal but prosaic, the poem could at first glance be regarded as sloppy compared to the poems in *Light*. But after the first two sentence units, spread over four lines and spaced widely from each other, the end, with the parallel motions and descriptors, and that final, not-quite-grammatical hyphen, itself recreates syntactically the tininess of the point of light, positioned in space as pure use value, ready to receive the smallest possible unit of ash. The whole process is crunched together into recognizably poetic language. There's a technique here that ranges across several things, rendering them especially minor given the magnitude of what they're taking in and the small amount of space in which they're able to do it, passing almost without our noticing.

Giovannone's work might seem entirely different from Thammavongsa's, but its detailed excavations of the obvious operate on a similar level. *The Nonnets*, named for the nine-line "sonnets" of which it's composed, extends the unique-sorta style of his debut, *The Loneliness Machine*. Like that collection, *The Nonnets* frequently breaks the fourth wall, speaking knowingly to whoever it is who makes up a contemporary Canadian poem's readership. (The opening poem ends, "Reader, you seem extraordinary.") That the book is simply a swath of nonnets—no sections, no table of contents, not even any titles beyond the fact that the first three words of each poem are capitalized—makes for an unselfconscious, seemingly genuine faith in its conceit. Giovannone's tweaking of the form is at once subtler than an augmentation like David McGimpsey's sixteen-line "chubby" variant and yet, due to its brevity, almost unrecognizable as a descendant of the sonnet. It's innovative in that it's understated; it's especially innovative in that most of us wouldn't at first recognize it as such.

The steady sweep of miniature triptychs variously creates syllogisms; shifts the sense of a word or idea; transitions from a lyric treatment of a theme to a discussion of said treatment to addressing a reader; or just tumbles in picaresque disjunction, as when "I Don't Drink Big Gulps" finds itself "At the Art Gallery of Ontario" for the second stanza and then begins the third, "I'm in the Portuguese Wine Club now!" Giovannone is really funny, but the consistency of his persona means that noticeable darkness or anger can also seep through. When "It's Hard to care" ends, "On Facebook, you seem to think / you're having fun, but you're not. / Not without me, you're not", the switch in register requires so little disruption of the goofy, self-effacing tone that the creepiness is off the charts. In "My Phone's GPS paused at a winery", the passive voice, along with the simplicity of Giovannone's form and conceit, brings out the totality of neo-liberal surveillance: "My credit card was charged // ninety-six dollars. / I know how this looks".

Unlike Thammavongsa's work or *The Nonnets*, Anstee's *Book of Annotations* self-consciously cycles through many different iterations of an aesthetic of tininess. It also reads like a meditation on modesty: even the book's measurements—seven by four-and-a-half inches—make it seem like only the humblest of upgrades from Anstee's sometimes tiny chapbook publications. And yet, there's a palpable compression, and concretism lurking within Anstee's minimalist exercises. The influence of Robert Lax is evident at several points. The untitled first poem, which repeats the lines

in rest
a pulse
beside
the eye

and then ends with the first two, draws attention (in what seems like the most direct way possible) to the experience of perception at the poem's core. Elsewhere, as in the four-word "Salvage", Anstee wrings multiple interpretations out of incredibly few elements: "each hour comes / apart". The erasure poems in the third section are themselves instances of compounded brevity. Basho's omnipresent haiku is plotted out only with six instances of the letter o; Lax's "the air" is reduced to "the", "and", "of", and two punctuation marks. Anstee's notes outline his methods, but the titles and blank spaces of the third section render explanation superfluous. Similarly, the method behind "Dissertation," a list of typos such as "hisotries / amterials / ripture", is almost immediately evident, as if Anstee's version of method-based or found poems exists in elementary particles. His miniature explorations, like Giovannone's hiding-in-plain-sight quirks and formal tweaks, are "minor" in a deliberate, holistic sense. They're also relatively free from self-conscious participation in any school or camp, their insistent minutiae rendering them as simply their own kind of poems.

Fleming's 2017 chapbook *The Worst Season* is also outwardly minimal, but, as its title suggests, it applies its minimalist engagements to a kind of ontological navigation of cyclical unhappiness. Perhaps reflecting the regular irregularity of ending-only-to-begin-again experiences of chronic health conditions, each page of the chapbook begins with an asterisk; the untitled poem that follows never quite manages to extend to the page's halfway point. There's this direct minimalism, but throughout it tries to capture the essence of something, with a fleeting image that never quite gets there. The first poem, one of the longer ones, begins, "I'm gaining frontiers", and, in its second and final stanza, builds the first of these inchoate metaphors:

> When I say I love you I mean
> I love this bird-self,
> something vital that isn't fight.
> Learn to hold at not knowing.

"I" appears too many times for a poem this short; "bird-self" creates a ghostly echo with "fight", which to me misread as "flight" at first glance; and then there's another resonance of "I" (lowercase) in "something vital that isn't flight", which immediately broadens into *o*, with closing line "Learn to hold at not knowing" containing within it a phono-visual approximation of two iambs, each shorter o sound followed by the long vowels in "hold" and "knowing". It's as if meter is dissolved and approximated in shifting assonance and the visual resonances of the vowels themselves.

The sense of uncertainty or provisionality that's at the centre of all experiences of being is brought out by the chapbook's titular conceit as it's reflected in recurring dialogues with a mental-health professional (*"How do you feel?"*, *"You said this is your worst season?"*, and *"Why aren't you happier?"*). It also partially emerges in another three-line offering:

> When I yawn I hear the knife sharpener's bell.
> Grief the thread behind the belly button
> pulled taut, puckering my upholstery.

It's the sublime in miniature, the poem's language "succeeding" insofar as it gives us something that can only ever jar—not the right image, and certainly not fulfilling its role even to whatever half-completion is required to participate as one of the lesser parts of an imaginary or potential allegory. The daily, barely or unspoken process of experiencing, trying to make sense and then not making sense of things is reflected all the more accurately because of the brevity.

Casteels' work possesses a similarly compressed totality. Rather than obliquely sketching a particular means of engagement, however, the prolific DIY publisher and writer instead produces a seemingly endless succession of in media res scenarios. I saw him read many times in Kingston, Ontario, and became used to the reliably odd, self-contained universes of his poems. Revisiting many of these pieces on the page, and at the distance of a few years, I find a strangely oral-as-written, lapidary quality, the roots of which extend much deeper than the poetic traditions drawn upon by the other poets in this chapter. Take as an example "Toenails and the Toes They Are Attached To", the first piece from what is, at the time of this writing, the most recent of Casteel's publications, *All We've Learned, Which Isn't Much* (2020), a collaborative work with Nicholas Papaxanthos:

> "Uh," said the dawn, then spat up
> a red wagon pulled behind an
> axe-murderer. 'It's all a dream!" I said
> but flames engulfed the mannequin factory,
> screams billowed like frosted death wind.

> Death is requesting a refund for the life that never arrived.

The title implies the kind of brief and yet comprehensive zooming-in on a small object or detail, as one finds in Thammavongsa's work. And yet, from the first word, we're thrust into a miniature world, the making of which exists in tandem with the narrative. The two are intertwined, neither able to exist without the other. Compare this with the most concise examples of George Fyler Townsend's translations of Aesop's *Fables*, like "The Hares and the Lions":

> The hares harangued the assembly, and argued that all should be equal. The Lions made this reply: "Your words, O Hares! are good; but they lack both claws and teeth such as we have."

Or, those that, like "The Hares and the Foxes", seem only slightly longer thanks to the addition of one-sentence paragraph summarizing the moral:

> The hares waged war with the Eagles, and called upon the Foxes to help them. They replied, "We would willingly have helped you, if we had not known who you were, and with whom you were fighting."

> Count the cost before you commit yourselves.

This elementary world-building, providing a didactic, epic-world sense of values in Aesop, is present in a necessarily smaller aesthetic dimension in Casteels and Papaxanthos' poems. What they give us is not life lessons as much as the smallest pieces of narrative—the first idea of a film treatment leaving off with itself.

Casteels' single-authored work packs in still more examples of smally singular stuff. *Still Lagoon*, published in 2017 on Casteels' own Puddles of Sky Press, is more substantial than his microchapbooks but, nevertheless, is compact in its twenty-four pages and 14-by-11-centimetre dimensions. It includes imagist snapshots ("When Downstairs Whispers, 'Shhh...'" consists of three lines: "A deep breath / inhales the person / who drops it"), Aesopian brevity ("Saint Frank" begins, "Upon leaving his humble abode he rode with a galloping gait to wait at the gate for entrance"), and Old Testament variations on the poet's almost slapdash construction of self-contained scenarios ("Cowslip Eclipse" kicks off, "Goliath hurled the sardine tin into the recycling bin").

The opening poem, "My Departure from Gallantry", is representative of much of Casteels' work, including much of the above plus a twist of perception, self-regard, and routine frozen in an image. Here it is in its entirety:

> The day began with a stone hefted through the lake's window. There was no piecing back my reflection. I was lagoon. Again and again I was lagoon. Nothing would change the simple fact that nothing would change the simple fact. It was very simple: everything had changed, and I was still lagoon.

Note the tie-in with not only the title of the chapbook, but the name of the press, itself something of an extension of Casteels' poetics. (His projects with Puddles of Sky include the journal *illiterature*, which has published issues comprised solely of, to take two especially innovative examples, one-word poems and rubber-stamped poems.) And yet the entire conceit is found not in Casteels' trade debut, *The Last White House at the End of the Row of White Houses* (2016), but a chapbook in an edition of 100, self-published in Kingston, each copy contained comic-book style in a plastic sleeve with matching dimensions. The visually disorienting repetition of "nothing would change the simple fact" itself draws attention to the format, reading as it does like an unintentionally reread or reprinted line in a forest of dense prose even as the small format and standard font size prevent the poem's 52 words from succumbing to this kind of confusion on the part of the reader.

It's so little, and yet it creates the illusion of excess—as the somewhat arbitrarily chosen list of titles included in this essay might indicate how much more of this little stuff could be cluttering up bookshelves and desk space anywhere one could expect poetry to be published. I also think it's no coincidence that I became familiar with Casteels' irreverent and yet lapidary minimalism through hearing it again and again and again, month after month at the open mic in Kingston. So while Deleuze and Guattari conclude that "There is nothing that is major or revolutionary except the minor", minimally oriented poetry seems to respond by easing into centre stage, taking with it and holding within itself the work it took to take even those small steps.

Formatting Engagement:
Small-Press Poetry Practices

To be a poet in North America is to enter the ranks of a perhaps unprecedented glut of literary creators. As Jed Rasula and Marjorie Perloff have pointed out, the numbers are staggering even when one considers merely the number of people teaching in creative writing programs at North American post-secondary institutions.[1] This inflationary system depends on perpetually expanding ranks of students; with it, one can expect an accompanying proliferation of alternative publishing methods. The supposedly legit side, involving MFAs and traditional publishing, grows loosely in proportion to even whatever publishing methods are, or were, seen as excluded, inferior, or just too weird.

This rise has already involved the proliferation of born-digital journals and magazines. Many don't last beyond a few issues, but, as following a few of them on Twitter reveals, this hasn't slowed what seems like exponential and unending growth. Try it: the recommended follows just keep coming, among them multiple magazines that have yet to publish a single issue. It's hard to view this phenomenon as sustainable, especially given

---

1   Perloff's "Poetry on the Brink: Reinventing the Lyric", published in the *Boston Review* in 2012, opens by referring to a "recent lecture" in which Rasula notes that there were at the time 458 institutions teaching creative writing, making for a faculty count of over 20,000, most of whom must publish in order to retain their positions.

that contemporary poetry's afterlife depends on whether it appears in literary criticism. Because of their digital provenance, these journals might very well be lost—not in the sense of being relegated to the library stacks or special collections (the fate of even the most obscure of defunct print journals), but in that it may never be possible to recover them at all.

For this reason, I want to suggest that there are other, often print-based, formats that might provide a way forward. Many of those that have persisted or found new life in the world of contemporary poetry have done so precisely because of their supposed obsolescence. It's this latter quality that creates further avenues of engagement within the participatory, and, at least potentially, insider-outsider relationships that structure contemporary poetry. Here are three.

I: The Chapbook

Perhaps the most notable format that works in tandem with the countless new digital journals is a more traditional print format that has nevertheless, thanks to its modesty, emerged reinvigorated, or at least newly proliferative. Enter the chapbook, the shabby format that seems likely to become still more visible than in DIY spells of the past. If describing the conventional poetry publishing routine using the allegory of the recording industry, one could regard the chapbook as the EP of the poetry world—a shorter offering that is at once demo and single or, after an artist has released a full-length, something that crops up between albums. Given the format's lower production costs, print runs, and expectations, however, as well as the ongoing strain on conventional poetry publishers, a more apt comparison would perhaps be the cassette. I don't mean the format's role as the portable alternative to mass-market LPs and CDs from the 1970s to '90s, but rather its persistence into the 2000s as the medium of choice for some experimental music communities in the US and elsewhere. As Nick Sylvester wrote on *Pitchfork* in 2013, the cassette, with its low sound quality and production costs, as well as its existence outside any kind of media hype, is perfectly suited to music that "doesn't feel desperate or needy or Possibly Important".

The cassette became the go-to format for extreme subgenres like power electronics and harsh noise. And yet, the reasons noise artists are drawn to the format—the improvisational nature of the music, extended length of single ideas, and resultant abundance of output—don't often apply to today's poets. Most of the chapbooks I read are far from the work of outlying radicals or misfits in the poetry landscape. Their authors seem to be playing the game, with the resonance I've detected born more of contemporary poetry's economic constraints. The chapbook is used to preview or hash out early ideas for longer projects that might later see publication in more conventional formats: see, for example, kevin mcpherson eckhoff's *Dissections from Their Biography*, published with above/ground press in 2012 and featuring examples of the biographical snippets that would be compiled into *Their Biography: an organism of relationships*, a trade collection published by Book*hug in 2015. Regardless, and at the risk of being unreasonably optimistic, I think the lowered expectations associated with the chapbook are productive in that they let their authors follow through on ideas that could seem either unwieldy if couched in a trade-length collection or, worse, half-baked if extended to that length.

The case can be illustrated by poets whose work seems to revolve entirely around this kind of format. For example, a small-press book like Cameron Anstee's *Book of Annotations*, discussed above, traffics in Anstee's extensive work in the chapbook format, with many of his publications being especially tiny (think, for instance, wallet-sized microchapbooks) and his trade-paperback upgrade mimicking this element of his poetic brand. It's not a coincidence that Anstee's poetics have found a home with Michael E. Casteels' Puddles of Sky Press, which recently issued *Words in Place*, a six-page microchapbook with dimensions of 2.5 by 2.25 inches.

But one can also find trade writers who have downgraded to a cassette-like format at least once since publishing elaborately produced books. Jordan Abel's *Timeless American Classic*, rendered in the recognizably rough aesthetics of rob mclennan's above/ground, employs some of Abel's eviscerating recombination-and-erasure technique, as seen in *The Place of Scraps* (2013), *Un/inhabited* (2014), and *Injun* (2016). The "Indian" pieces (numbered one through nine and staggered throughout the chapbook) work as an alternate iteration of *Injun*'s Notes section, in which a single keyword (examples include whitest, frontier, discovery, and warpath) appears on successive lines, aligned in the center of each, with preceding text from the source to the left of the keyword and subsequent text on the right. In *Injun*, each keyword fits seamlessly into the spacing of the swaths of found text, with the central column visually emphasized using darker text. *Timeless American Classic*, however, sets the keyword off from surrounding text using a blank column on either side:

so much obscurity in the	Indian	traditions, and so much confusion
so much confusion in the	Indian	names, as to render some
it. the color of the	Indian	the writer believes, is peculiar
latter. The imagery of the	Indian	both in his poetry and
experience; but the North American	Indian	clothes this ideas in a

This simpler, typographically jarring iteration of one of the central arrangements of *Injun* foregrounds the method behind such pieces as well as the chapbook's lower production quality. There's a physicality in these pieces that's comparatively absent in the slick typographical innovations of Abel's trade publications.

Abel's immense success (he won the 2017 Griffin Poetry Prize as well as numerous other awards, including the 2014 Dorothy Livesay Poetry Prize) puts him at odds with the struggling-artist landscape I've outlined. Still, *Timeless American Classic* seems like both an outlet for Abel's abundance of ideas as well as a venue to explore his experiences as a scholar who is familiar with the Digital Humanities. Data-visualization techniques are especially evident in the "Topic" pieces, which consist of clusters of variously sized keywords. Regardless of the reasons behind or resonances of Abel's approach, however, *Timeless American Classic* is a fascinating minor text by one of Canada's most vital and consistently rewarding poets.

Andy Verboom's *Orthric Sonnets* (2017) features a more traditional but no less singular conceit, rendered in an elaborate edition from London's Baseline Press that measures 5.75 by 7.5 inches, includes thirty-six pages, and exists in an edition of only sixty. Its title refers to the two-headed dog Orthrus from Greek mythology. The chapbook's notes describe Soviet physician Vladimir Demikhov's transplantation experiments, which included attaching the top half of one dog, Shavka, to the body and circulatory system of another, Brodyaga. Accordingly, Verboom's thirteen quasi-sonnets—eleven of which consist of fourteen lines followed by twelve more on the facing page—reflect not even hybridity as much as a crude, cruel reduction of two into something just less than.

Orthric Sonnets uses this imagery to explore such experiments as well as the artifice of poetry, as in "Creating a Two-Headed Dog through Extraordinary Surgical Skill":

> It doesn't require a perversion
> to demand this exotic bend
> in what dogs are and how they're spent.
> Soon, our bodies will be blank verse.

Many of the poems employ abstruse terminology; in others, subtler formal oddities are the stitches holding the poems together. The final one, written after Soviet scientist Sergei Brukhonenko, in its closing stanza repeats the latter's name, subsequently splicing flamboyant wordplay with ESL solecism: "She will never again flamenco. / The wife, I mean, not dog you caught".

Verboom's style can be dense, but here it's tightened a bit, or minimized, into a kind of formalist swagger. The twelve-line opener "Envying", for example, flashes through a take on another disorienting metamorphosis: "we could exchange our sexes. Simple. / Vow a slapped-fat-tick's worth of not / never or always, a well-pocked / pact". This improvement is especially welcome given that one could imagine Verboom's subject matter being especially susceptible to a kind of prog-lyrics blend of verbosity and sci-fi cartoonishness.

Instead, the brevity of the chapbook format brings out another kind of density: that is, the distillation of all that strange background reading into a brief run of high-quality poems. The idea would likely have been tiresome as a full book, or even a slightly longer cycle shoehorned into one. Here, though, the oddness is compressed into a strange richness; a reader may even get the impression that it's all stuffed into a package a little too short to do the idea justice.

Tess Liem's *Tell everybody I say hi* (Anstruther Press, 2017) is more fragmented. It reads like a sampling of variations on minimalist lyric and Language writing influences, reducing them so that the chapbook's thirteen pages of poetry express the quotidian performativities that fill our days.

Accordingly, Liem at once engages with and voids the loaded categorizations and identity markers that inhere in the lyric self. The first poem signals as much with its title ("I, a compartment"), which reappears at the end of the quick succession of first-person pronouns that begin the poem:

> I count keepsakes
> when I can't sleep.
>
> I, a compartment & careful,
> invite you into hallways.

"Saw in half" uses a palindromic form to collapse repetition and incompleteness into a disarming unity, with the central line, "proof: a body can be OK divided, too", holding together reversible sequences like "actually a navy blue. / Under the saw she is / one whole night divided in two". "Everything I do is political, especially when we stay home" packs quandaries about the personal, political, and performative into the comforts of closed space: "We stay in / & keep our bodies ethical // so to speak. We know if we go out, / we will dress for the street". Again, the politicized and the inane become as interchangeable as relatable.

Liem's poems often seem truncated or clipped, as though they're reducing the particularity of experience to quotidian acts like procrastinating and people-watching, usually providing just enough to articulate this truncation as well as mimic it formally. "Wish for sleep" and "New Superstitions" are point-form lists, each ending with an italicized conclusion that seems to signal the end of a poet's pre-writing stage and beginning of a hypothetical poem. (The latter ends, "- write a note to yourself: // *I, too, am capable of being unkind / like a wasp*".) The result is a quick cycle of vignettes illustrating selves that are often as half-formed as much as they're in flux. It's quotidian to the point of being half-finished, the modest chapbook format creating and justifying the effect.

The kinds of brevity employed in all these examples are replicated in the quickness of the reading process as well as many chapbooks' very low print runs. If the appeal of the chapbook is indeed a symptom of Canadian poetry's supply-side glut, one can only hope the format's concision also predicts the impending end of the era of cutbacks that produced these bleak conditions. On the other hand, and regardless of whether one's on board with that reading, I hope it doesn't also anticipate any end to younger Canadian poets' abundance of weird, great poetry-thing ideas.

II: The Subscription
Another should-have-died-by-now idea that has found new life in contemporary poetry is the print subscription. Some subjective, thick-ish description: my first ever magazine subscription was *Nintendo Power,* and the most recent was *Poetry.* But this doesn't count the several poetry-related publications I'm receiving at any given time in return for writing or as a consolation prize after entering a contest (or the ones I sporadically look through in the library's current-periodicals section). Contemporary poetry has a strange relationship with subscriptions; with most of its readership seeming to consist of those also plying their trade in Canada's far-from-lucrative poetry universe, the circulation of its publications may not reflect readership as much as the number of people submitting their work. Sure, the arrangement is more participatory than *The New Yorker*'s business model, or even more of a game—maybe I haven't come so far from my *Nintendo Power* days—but it's also something of a closed system.

North Vancouver's The Alfred Gustav Press has managed to find a unique place for itself in this ecosystem. Founded by poet David Zieroth, every year it publishes two series, each consisting of three chapbooks and a "holm", the latter being a brief offering (or "small island in the river", according to its colophon) by a poet who has previously published with the press. Each series must be ordered in advance, and the press prints as many copies as there are subscribers. The four-title packages invoke sameness and difference, the beige of each cover adorned only with the author's signature and a small, consistently idiosyncratic two-colour "icon" drawn by Zieroth.

One of the complete series I have in my possession, Series Nineteen (published in June 2018), features thematic resonances and textual innovations that unfold within recognizable publication standards. The series includes John Wall Barger's *Dying in Dharamsala*, Claudia Coutu Radmore's *On Fogo,* and Michael Trussler's *Light's Alibi,* as well as an eight-page holm by Russell Thornton entitled *Aftermath.* (Thornton's *Stopping the Waves* appeared in the previous series.) Each of the three chapbooks engages with experiences of travel, with Barger in India's Himachal Pradesh, Radmore having travelled to the island of Fogo, off the coast of Newfoundland, and Trussler reflecting on journeys to the Kunsthistorisches Museum in Vienna and the site of Mauthausen, a Nazi concentration camp. There's a just barely unified theme, but even detecting that trace of unity feels contrived. A series like this doesn't need to espouse an overt thematic, just as one doesn't tend to subscribe to a journal or magazine and expect a special or themed issue every time around. Instead, each iteration can create a space in which poets can generate singularly ambitious works that are nevertheless conscious of their smaller stature and existence as a grouping—characteristics that might be regarded as limitations but which the series uses as strengths, all the while slightly increasing the number of voices at play in a vaguely book-priced offering.

Dying in Dharamsala purports to show us the poet, "rattled and heartsick" and "attempting not to look away". Barger has a way with line breaks, which here add a formal element to his visual conceit. The eponymous poem that opens the chapbook tweaks a familiar line-as-single-breath poetics to construct a delusion in which "Luiz lies upon his many mats"

> to invite us into a realm
> where he is not sick
> where he has cured himself
> with tinctures.
> And we believe it
> how could we not believe it?

"Cryptoscopophilia" twists things still a bit tighter in this respect, multiplying its line breaks to capture the experience of peripheral vision, complete with hues of voyeurism and shame:

> it is our business
> look away
> white dude.
> The boy teeters
> water's edge
> his light dim
> fluttering. I look
> I can't help it
> through the mist window
> and the goblins
> spot me
> they scramble out
> in every
> direction.

Barger tends to write either travelogue-style works or else extended treatments of the truly bizarre, such as the baffling *The Book of Festus* (2015) or *The Vnfortunate Report & Tragicall Tidings of Leslie Barger* (2016), a chapbook that manages the unlikely feat of revitalizing and further deconstructing historiographically inclined poetry. In reducing travel narrative into a series of perception-obsessed vignettes, *Dying in Dharamsala* reads like a formally tight synthesis of Barger's work to date. It matches Alfred Gustav's format in that it might work also as an introduction point to his work, creating and sustaining interest in it just as it might bring existing readers into the constellation of those aware of the press' work—a readership that is in many cases also a writership.

Radmore's *On Fogo* takes a step away from her Language-inflected work with haiku and other Japanese forms in favour of more directly rendering a particular setting. In opener "Sea Oyster Leaf, Sea Olive: Fogo", proper nouns and other specificities are scattered throughout its descriptions: "no fanfare, but the bulletin board poster, hand- // lettered on card, says The Ace i' coming to Fogo / on the 30th, and everyone is invited".

Several of the poems consist of long sentences div² two-, three-, or four-line stanzas. On the surface, t¹ very different from the exacting concision of much of Radmore's work. Still, many of the formal flourishes seem ready to burst in their compactness, like when "Berry Grounds" sketches outcroppings and patches of colour via brief swaths of repetition:

> and you dream at night of more berries and dottings
> of butter-and-eggs in the grass and berries and butter-
> and-eggs tucked in from the wind and there's your patch

> and her patch and his patch, you're not done till you've
> scoured all the green you can see, till the wind knocks
> you back toward small ponds stocked with clouds[.]

Despite their prosaic nature, it's difficult to excerpt an entire grammatical sentence from many of these poems—their length and sprawling enjambment themselves get at a sort of raggedness of experience and perception.

Radmore's notes about the reading tour that brought her to Fogo recall the tactility in many of the poems. "The landscape invited touch", she writes; "It required attention, wanted to be heard". She then describes her desire to "record every single thing", including her conversations with "other travellers as they shared experiences not accessible to me, like the Beau's Beer crew that was trying to get a 'taste' of Fogo Island into one of their '150' series of brewings". It's a relatable instance of trying to relate to people trying to relate to something authentic; that the poems the trip produced have appeared on a subscription-based press itself keeps Radmore's fragments of Fogo just a little safer from whatever authenticity-thirsty poetry-tourists may be out there.

Trussler, too, works around the edges of established formats. His short fiction and poetry frequently delve into those on the margins of aspiring, middle-class society, even if they do so from he perspective of the writer-professor. Trussler's snapshots of universe also have a multimedia element: his conventional frequently engages with the medium of photography, *emade Life* (2009) consists of photographs as well as n a series of similarly sized postcards. *Alibi* engage directly with specific paintings, Trussler's keen eye for photographic of light and colour. "They've Never

Smelled Jet Fuel" does both, describing a green that is "in only one place, stays inside a room in Vienna", and which

> we can at least gape at underneath this rizzened
> green that scores cuts in a pond's ice
> made by skaters and how bark feels unlike
> snow in the hands.

Trussler's note identifies the painting as *Hunters in the Snow*, adding that "'rizzened' is of my own invention: Bruegel's unusual green seems to call for a new word". The poem is steeped in high art without seeming abstruse; subsequent comparisons, including "like finding / Japanese green tea picked in the springtime and within this bounty", carry the reader's eye away from the implied object and deep into formally resonant associations.

The chapbook's unique formatting lets Trussler weave space and pace into his exploration of perception. Each poem is printed sideways, prompting readers to tilt the book ninety degrees clockwise and turn the pages from bottom to top rather than right to left. This layout is used to particular advantage in "Jet Fuel", which slows down already-long lines with abundant white space, and "To My First Love", which describes sporadic communications with the addressee and gradually becomes more long-winded, its lines lengthening well past what the other chapbooks' layout would accommodate: "But jealousy I knew, that unimaginable addiction, that blindfold pressed closer / than waking up tomorrow, before you took it with you, jealousy I mean". This has been done before, of course. Still, the variation on a formerly experimental touchstone works within the series format—it works within the standardization implied in the artwork and length of each entry in the series while also standing out as different, preventing the four offerings from seeming like interchangeable components of the package.

In comparison with Trussler's sweeping entry, Thornton's brief *Aftermath* seems especially packed-in, its smaller dimensions and typeface accommodating three long-ish poems and one eight-part prose piece. In contrast with the series' focus on travel, Thornton stays close to his (and Alfred Gustav's) home of North Vancouver. Proper nouns frequently locate the poems here, but it's perhaps "The Water and the Stone Trap"—the most unmarked of the quartet—in which Thornton's hypnotic, subtly changing repetitions invoke the expected unexpectedness of home:

> The work of the rocks is to gather all the water
> the way the people here once gathered fish after silver-scaled fish.
> The rocks collect the water, and the water collects the rocks—
> there is nothing else for either the water or the rocks.

Thornton's identifiable style both increases the thematic resonances of the series and reflects the longer-term continuity the holm feature lends to Alfred Gustav. And yet one of the things that makes the press so unique also undercuts this kind of consistency. In being subscription based, there's no way, at least officially, to go back and purchase a title you missed. This is a strange reversal of sorts, given that most of the remaining print literary journals—however niche—make back issues available at a discounted price. The press is ensconced in the boutique market we've come to associate with poetry, and yet it manages to create scarcity and exclusivity in an industry already working on such a small scale that presses, micro- and otherwise, often offer complete annual subscriptions. (Try to imagine similar packages being offered by "major" record labels, or even mid-sized publishers of fiction.)

Zieroth writes on the press' website that he thinks of Alfred Gustav's readership as "small but intense", and that the press is "an effort of guild-like pleasure keen to bring poetry to readers". Both statements indicate that the publisher exists firmly within the ever-retrenching universe of poetry publishing. But it also succeeds in carving out a space within that environment and giving its poets room to breathe and to generate rarities, even if the idea of a poetry-related curio at this point verges on redundancy. It's conscious of its limitations to the extent that it uses them as strengths; in the process, perhaps it can help expand that universe by inviting those on its edges just a little further inside.

III: The Dispersion

My recent experience as part of an English-language poetry community in Wuhan, China, bears out these developments. It also, despite the extreme specificity of the situation, extrapolates the above factors, perhaps providing a glimpse of poetry's possible futures in the West.

As Guriel wrote in an essay revisiting Roald Dahl's "Lucky Break", a piece on his serendipitous initiation into the vocation of writer, "No one accidentally discovers that they're a writer anymore; they simply *decide* they are a writer, and then invite you to their book launch". Guriel's beef here seems to be that the notion that writing well is a talent one either has or doesn't is now regarded as outdated, perhaps owing to our cultural moment's ascendant blank-slate belief—that, in the absence of systemic oppressions, each of us can be whatever we choose. (Guriel ventriloquizes the hypothetical case against Dahl's faith in lucky breaks thus: "Any meathead with a graduate degree could make meat pie out of the Englishman who wrote 'Lucky Break'; they would point out that Dahl [white, straight, male, and privileged] had the luxury to let lucky breaks happen".) It's increasingly commonplace to quibble with the difficulties dead people once thought they'd had, and it's also true that one can present oneself as a writer on Twitter. But is it really true that writerdom in any meaningful sense is so easy an existence to choose?

Almost anyone can self-publish; they can also self-distribute, at least to whatever extent their social life includes something resembling face-to-face interactions with other human beings. This has always been the case, but I want to suggest again that poetry is distinct in some way, and that, as the economics behind the form seem bound to get worse and worse, there will be creative forms of retrenchment that might allow poets and publishers to soldier on while also retaining the potentiality of the social and artistic configurations I've been exploring.

Subscriptions in poetry are, of course, like most of the ostensibly novel cultural formations explored in this book, not entirely new. Edward Hartley Dewart, another poetry curator working amid a dearth of resources (if less of a public disinterest in poetry), navigated the ephemerality of poems-by-subscription when putting together *Selections from Canadian Poets with Occasional Critical and Biographical Notes and an Introductory Essay on Canadian Poetry* (1864), the first Canadian poetry anthology. Dewart faced a unique problem. As Douglas Lochhead's introduction to the 1973 reprint puts it,

> Dewart recognized that he was living in a time of unprecedented newspaper publication and that much poetry which he read would never appear again unless he played the role of rescuer. His role was clear. He did indeed save many poems from oblivion, but it is only right to point out that in those nineteenth-century newspapers and periodicals which have survived there are many poems still to be collected and given the attention they deserve.

Dewart himself discusses the problem explicitly in one of the scattered (and sometimes lengthy) discursive footnotes one finds throughout the collection. He notes that John Breakenridge's "The Passage of the Beresina" was "From '*The Crusades and other Poems*'", published "by subscription at Kingston in 1846". Praising the longer work as possessing "considerable poetic merit, though portions of it are somewhat prosaic and diffuse in style", he finishes, "The volume is probably now out of print". The subscription format perhaps making finding it that much more of a lost cause, Lochhead's commentary on the matter construes the means of distribution as being perhaps another quirk or complication in the archival labour of finding work from the period.

Surveying what English-language poetry communities and institutions I came across while living in central China, I found a few different types and accompanying formats. Expectedly, the big cities, Shanghai and Beijing, had more relevant outlets, with contributor bios that included world-class university affiliations and high-prestige publication credits. Entities in second-tier cities like Hangzhou and Wuhan, where I lived, tended to have yearly releases, some of which were open to submissions in some capacity. Still, this format tended to reward regular participants with publication of one or more poems presented or workshopped throughout the year. In the context of English-language poetry communities scattered over vast distances in various provincial capitals of China, the system appeared to work well—it encouraged participation, built and made a record of communities, and, given the obscurity, limited print runs, and haphazard distributional methods, never languished as a markedly amateur venue. (I never encountered a Wuhan poet who poo-pooed at the idea of having something included in *Earshrub*, the zine Osmanthus sporadically published.)

Shoddy or obsolete publishing formats were certainly playing a role in all this. There were odd formatting and production choices in at least two of the publications we encountered, one of which looked a lot like a high-school yearbook. Most people seemed to have been making it up as they went. (We certainly were with Osmanthus.) Osmanthus has ended a few seasons now with basic printouts made out of stock we found at print shops or online. These weren't aesthetic choices as much as necessities; in a sense, we were working backwards from the conscious aesthetic choices of something like derek beaulieu's No Press, or even jwcurry's later productions—coming out of kitsch or deliberate obsolescence to recreate in a tech-obsessed environment some fabled DIY era of real scarcity and real resourcefulness. Despite some bicultural and bilingual participation, there didn't always seem to be much precedent for the North American-style small presses and reading series. While contemporary Canadian small poetry presses like The Blasted Tree and Ryan Fitzpatrick's Model Press have a similarly dispersed, dislocated quality (Fitzpatrick's PDF chapbook publications list their location as "Toronto/Tkaronto, for now"), these entities are nevertheless embedded in a more familiar landscape of affiliations. We were figuring things out in a place where there wasn't much English, working with spatially disparate units of people, coming from different parts of the world, who often had no knowledge of each other or their work. It was within this dynamic that we were trying to negotiate with print-shop owners in Mandarin and figure out how to make a Chinese-language home printer give us the format we needed. The chapbooks we released had no ISBNs; many individual copies didn't even have smooth edges or binding that held. But it worked, until the pandemic happened and everything scattered to the winds.

Jim Shepard's affirming 2019 defence of literary journals in *Literary Hub* inadvertently hits on this central paradox: "Almost certainly more than any other media in our country", Shepard writes, "literary magazines model critical thinking and arrange an exposure to the unorthodox, both of which can provide inoculations against where we seem to be headed as a collective. They assist in that crucial rear-guard holding action on both reading and writing's behalf". Education and public life are certainly being systematically gutted, and the pandemic is likely to make this worse. Exposure to new ideas and experiences is valuable; of course reading is good. But the tension Shepard notes between agreed-upon arrangement and the ostensibly unorthodox calls into question the extent to which novelty can truly exist in any culture or subculture established enough to have a (however dwindling) architecture in which medium, small, and smaller formats vie for what supposedly little attention is still available to us. Perhaps, in order to move forward, we'll have to look still further backwards.

"Whatever she is, she is not nothing": *Recuperating Rupi Kaur*

Our cultural life sometimes seems to consist of a constant churning of album reissues, abortive first-novel manuscripts published posthumously, critical editions, and much-needed reassessments. It's a pop-culture manifestation of a trend Paul Mann wrote about in *The Theory-Death of the Avant-Garde* (1991)—that is, that the relationship between the avant-garde and academy has resulted in the perpetual "recuperation" of margins, born of a fundamentally late-capitalist urge to "discursively engage" with and thus coopt the excluded. What was once deemed inferior, or uninteresting, or just uncool can inevitably be recontextualized, mined for meaning, or relocated in our ever-evolving—ever assimilating—repertoire of cultural stuff. Mann characterized the avant-garde as "the production of a death-theory, a seemingly inexhaustible discourse of exhaustion" located within the university system's perpetual present, in which the "performance immediacy" of just about any work lives on in scholarly description. Lately, the chatter might be more ephemeral, but the dynamic seems to us less like death-theory and more like just life.

I sometimes wonder how far we can follow Mann's line of thinking—will this phenomenon someday extend to discourses of racism or other bigotries? Less hard to imagine is a widespread rehabilitation of poetry as a popularly read genre. While few would argue that this has occurred, the form has found new popularity thanks to accessible writers who take cues from social media. Rupi Kaur—whose work I'm not exactly a fan of—has been at the forefront of this movement, having sold more than eight million books and been translated into over forty languages. These aren't just poetry-world heights: Kaur is a star by any standard.

Kaur also seems to be undergoing a recuperation closer to that discussed by Mann. While her greeting-card verse hasn't gotten much critical attention, there are indications of a turnaround. Visible among tangential remarks and social media following lists if not as many direct statements, this gradual warming to Kaur seizes on her straightforwardly signifying style, which remains free from the aloofness that, in the popular imagination, characterizes poetry. Instead, Kaur's work expresses a participatory element that I think remains unique to poetry and its readership, even at a time when the literary arts seem less lucrative or sustainable than ever.

Despite initially having been met with widespread critical scorn, the work of Kaur has recently been described by respected Canadian poet Souvankham Thammavongsa as throwing rules out the window and demonstrating that "[e]verything I had ever been told about [poetry], she proves it's not true, you don't have to be that or go that way". "Whatever she is", Thammavongsa continues, "she is not nothing". There's certainly something to this singularity-in-simplicity. Kaur's debut especially, *Milk and Honey* (2014), reflects and narrates this learning process by deconstructing the fundamental stylistic conventions of lyric poetry. Here's what I mean:

> i can't tell if my mother is
> terrified or in love with
> my father it all
> looks the same[.]

One doesn't find those popular understandings of a line as a grammatical unit or "a breath"—even the sense of a pause that would be signified in prose with a sentence break or semicolon ("my father; it all") is collapsed. The lines are arranged not for a trained eye, but to achieve the baseline status of just being identifiable as a poem.

The so-called crisis in poetry's readership has in fact always been with us. Restricted to a niche market at best, kept on life support by the neoliberal university system and self-congratulatory prize culture, poetry is produced and distributed thanks to grant money blinking out in the increasing darkness of austerity. The endlessly self-reflexive "end of poetry" is handily summed up by Kathryn Mockler's self-reflexive prose poem "Poetry—You're Popular, Okay", which puts the case thus: "I don't know why you care so much about what other people think or do. Why do you need everyone to be your friend?" and concludes, "Take a break. Take some time off once in a while and go all the way around to the back of the school to the pit where the kids go when they skip class and where they like to get stoned".

Mockler is a traditional Canadian print poet, whose work is regarded as operating in a minor genre even compared to the literary fiction on which such small presses tend to shine more of their limited spotlight. The poetry produced by Kaur, in contrast, is most definitely, unequivocally, unironically, very popular. It's likely because of this lack of cred, along with the lack of convention, that Kaur's work has prompted some takedowns. UK poet Rebecca Watts, as part of a somewhat reactionary take on the similarly popular Hollie McNish, includes Kaur in her query about why the poetry world is "pretending that poetry is not an art form?" Criticizing the valorization of honesty and accessibility at the expense of craft and "intellectual engagement", Watts describes what is essentially a simplified confessionalism in which "honesty is defined as the constant expression of what one feels, and accessibility means the complete rejection of complexity, subtlety, eloquence and the aspiration to do anything well".

Watts' piece channels a markedly British form of identity politics backlash—she sees the trend as sustained by a "middle-aged, middle-class reviewing sector" that is "terrified of being seen to disparage the output of young, self-styled 'working-class' artists", subsequently linking this to a more transatlantic trend of finding value in demographic representation over and above whatever substance ostensibly used to be found in the words themselves. And yet—recall, for a moment, my appreciation for the negative review's ignition points for further inquiry—at one point in the article, Watts identifies something that I think is likely more central to the appeal of poets like Kaur. This comes as part of her lament over the death of expertise, which includes the caveat that

> There is an upside to poetry becoming something that 'anyone could do'. The art form can no longer be accused of being elitist— an accusation that until recently has precluded its mass-market appeal. In other contexts, elitism is not considered an evil in itself. We frankly desire our doctors, hairdressers, plumbers and sportspersons to be the best: to learn from precedent, work hard, hone their skills and be better than we are at their chosen vocations. Even in the other arts, the line between amateur and professional is clearer than it is in poetry.

Descendant of the working man that I am, I agree that hard work and sharpened skill are the values that matter when it comes to hairdressers and plumbers. Leaving aside the sum total of the "other arts", as part of what I'm arguing here, I think poetry is different— not in that anyone can do it, but rather because the expansive, open-to-the-world quality that attracts precisely this type of engagement (trying, doing, critiquing, debriefing, or even dismissing) is part of what matters. We know that contemporary poetry is mostly for people who write poetry. Whatever you think of Kaur's poems themselves, the fact that she exists as part of this same world, with her wide and educative appeal, shows that poetry's self-contained nature isn't always the same thing as elitism.

Relatedly, a 2017 profile in *The Guardian* sums up Kaur's appeal fairly well: her style, like that of other prominent Instapoets, consists of "rupturing short confessional pieces with erratic line breaks to share hard-won truths" (Khaira-Hanks). The article ends with a valid point about snobbery—that, "like many pop musicians before her, she commits the sin of engaging with a demographic whose taste is often seen as a byword for bad quality"—but it just as quickly swerves from the poetry itself and into the issues of demographic representation that have taken over so much literary discourse:

> As a young woman of colour in a world where white, male delectations are treated as the definitive barometer of taste, Kaur speaks a truth that the literary establishment is unlikely to understand. Even the

sincerest critique of her work can slide from healthy debate into vicious attack at the turn of a page. But to read Kaur's success as an omen of the death of poetry would be to unfairly dismiss writing that contains bravery, beauty and wisdom. Frankly, the literary world is saturated with white male voices of dubious quality. Kaur's poetry should be given the same freedom to be flawed.

Support for Kaur has also come from predictable scholarly calls to destabilize twentieth-century notions of literariness, defined both stylistically and demographically. David McQuillan's 2018 MA thesis on the "Subversive Simplicity" of Kaur's work argues that the controversy around Kaur involves "the cultural legacies and aesthetic priorities of twentieth-century high modernism, which privilege difficulty in literature above all other reading practices". That Kaur privileges "simplicity and accessibility over complexity and difficulty" is, according to this academically approved approach, a logical part of her experience as a poet of colour who immigrated to Canada early in life and has faced the "potentially alienating factors" of the association of literary difficulty with High Modernism and, by extension, the whiteness of its practitioners.

Kaur's identity as a woman of colour certainly explains some of her appeal, as well as some of the controversy surrounding her work. But what seems a more likely reason for her success is her verse's unpretentious, social-media-oriented forms of address, as well as her arrangement of these elements into book-length offerings that beckon to prospective readers and writers of poetry. It's minimal but in an unadorned sense—one that remains free from the studied or stylized connotations of the term. Kaur's is a looser, more conversational and, crucially, more immediately recognizable poetic language that replaces image, symbol, and formal arrangement with more directly signifying references to narrative and reflective content, the act of writing poetry, and the real-life print forms on which such poetry might be composed and in which they may appear for whoever apprehends them.

In fact, I think the "poetry is read only by poets" paradigm is central to the enormous appeal of Kaur's work. Perhaps because of the endlessly expanding constellation of topics, genres, and forms that our culture recuperates as the stuff of culture and commentary, as well as Kaur's dialogue with the expressive formats of social media, her work addresses an unprecedently large audience of ostensible insiders. Her work is downstream from the quiet, older-millennial revolts against the selfie that seem almost quaintly a part of contained teenaged alienation and rebellion and that register as irrelevant now. One such moment that sticks in my mind is the faux 2013 controversy in *Rolling Stone*, recycled by *Pitchfork* in their then-section Echo Chamber, when Vampire Weekend singer Ezra Koenig (b. 1984) made the following complaints, compiled from quotations available in both articles:

> I'm definitely pro-selfie. I think that anybody who's anti-selfie is really just a hater. Because, truthfully, why shouldn't people take pictures of themselves? When I'm on Instagram and I see that somebody took a picture of themselves, I'm like, "Thank you." I don't need to see a picture of the sky, the trees, plants. There's only one you. I could Google image search "the sky" and I would probably see beautiful images to knock my socks off. But I can't Google, you know, "What does my friend look like today?" For you to be able to take a picture of yourself that you feel good enough about to share with the world—I think that's a great thing. There's all this bullshit about "the younger kids today are more self-absorbed." It's like, give me a fucking break! I've been in nursing homes, where my grandma is. I've seen some of the most selfish people on the planet in there... And the world that these kids are born into literally could not get more selfish. The world is so fucked-up and unequal and full of assholes. You can't blame it on the younger generation.[1]

The selfie as worthwhile seems to be the consensus, but what about the quieter people who don't fit? Kaur (b. 1992) is uniquely positioned to recalibrate this angst in a way that accommodates contemporary poetry's niche market. Down to the design of her print editions, she fuses this perennial anxiety with the social elements of the Internet. Kaur's poems are selfies for people who were uncomfortable with selfies.

This progression from reading to writing to publishing is built into the format of *Milk and Honey*. Its first untitled section

---

1   See Vozick-Levison and Battan, respectively, for the *Rolling Stone* and *Pitchfork* pieces from which the series of quotations is drawn.

of text that is recognizable as a standalone lyric poem (following the epigraph and before the table of contents) reads,

> my heart woke me crying last night
> *how can i help* i begged
> my heart said
> *write the book*[.]

An educative element manifests in the form of the print book and the reader's progression through that book, creating a social-media-time *Künstlerroman*—a version of the *Bildungsroman*, or a novel about one's education or coming of age, that ends with the socialization of the inexperienced or alienated individual. What makes the *Künstlerroman* different, and more applicable to *Milk and Honey*, is that it also traces the progress of an artist, often culminating in the development of the narratively described subject into the author of the text itself—so, a kind of multimodal socialization, with the narratively described world as well as its larger realm of existence finding expression in the relationship between reader and text. If the only people who read poetry are poets, Kaur's poetry might be for people just opening up to that possibility.

This dynamic of participation and writerly growth is nothing new in Canadian poetry. Rob Taylor's contributor reflection in *Beyond Forgetting: Celebrating 100 Years of Al Purdy* (2018) brings this dynamic into clearer focus. Taylor states that Al Purdy was the first contemporary poet in Canada he discovered: "His poems, and his personal history, made me believe it was possible that a Canadian kid with no immediately discernible talent could eventually make it if he worked hard enough". Taylor's *What the Poets Are Doing: Canadian Poets in Conversation*, also published in 2018, is where one finds Thammavongsa's praise. Kaur "is not nothing" in that she "means something to me because once when I had mentioned I was a Canadian poet, I was told, 'That's nothing'. I was so humiliated for having thought myself one and then humiliated because I didn't say anything back because of the possibility that maybe it was a valid point about me". Thammavongsa suggests that Kaur's poetry deconstructs the mores of good taste and is thus anti-elitist. Kaur is for people who don't explicitly make the leap into "I want to be a poet" the way

Taylor and his readership do. Her poetic practice resonates with their contemplation of whether they could write poetry—a process that begins with the question of whether one can read poetry.

Thammavongsa's remarks resonate with another sentiment expressed in Taylor's brief comment in *Beyond Forgetting*: that Purdy's writing inspired him such that "I've worked, reading Al along the way, my writing going where it's needed to go, but also swinging back in its orbit toward Al from time to time". The interactive appeal in Kaur—that which inspired Thammavongsa to just keep doing whatever kind of writing was her "way"—is manifest here as a further participatory element, the Al Purdy A-Frame Residency. Being a recipient of this fellowship means that Taylor has "lived in the A-frame and gotten to know Eurithe", Purdy's own social circle persisting in the personal and professional development Taylor describes to a likely even greater extent than do many of those early poems he read.

I have no idea if Kaur will occupy any comparable position in the future of Canadian poetry. I do think that Kaur's work does document a journey of its own: from hailing social media's sensitive rebels, to initiating potential readers and subsequent writers of poetry, to demonstrating with the unfolding form of her books themselves her own attainment of the position of published author.

Subsequent poems in her debut feature elementary, conversational renderings of connotation, figures of speech, and similarly quotidian, often spoken "literary" devices. One poem, in its entirety, reads, "*i've had sex* she said / but i don't know / what making love / feels like". A poem like this is educative in that it explores the shades of precision and connotation that distinguish literal phrasings ("have sex") from more figurative or implication-rich (although still colloquial) alternatives ("make love").

Kaur makes frequent use of familiar print conventions, especially from prose and dramatic texts, to gently, gradually ease readers into the concept of "poetic" language. This obtains in her line breaks as well. To return to one of the poems in the section "the hurting"—"i can't tell if my mother is / terrified or in love with / my father it all / looks the same"—we find disregarded entirely not only the commonly recognized line break but punctuation as well. This more generalized lack of convention, in which "is terrified" straddles a line break but "my father it all" exists unpunctuated within a line, blurs together perception and emotion, formally reflecting, or, in the context of free verse, even narrativizing uncertainty and the isolation of the feeling subject.

Hence the journey in *Milk and Honey* towards the manifestation of these successive realizations in the form of the published book. Further stages of this journey include Kaur's use of familiar prose and dramatic techniques to gently ease readers into the concept of "poetic" language:

> you whisper
> *i love you*
> what you mean is
> *i don't want you to leave*

She reverses poetry's complicating role, using the medium to demystify distinctions between what we want and what we need. The poems fumble for what might be the first time with identifiably poetic language, expressing their linguistic discoveries in the almost-metaphor that bubbles up from stale wordplay:

> the night after you left
> i woke up so broken
> the only place to put the pieces
> were the bags under my eyes

The book consists not so much of a series of similar revelations but as several intertwined ones that gradually develop. The past-its-expiry-date relationship of the above passage, for instance, gets a somewhat more comprehensive, more articulate treatment further along in the section:

> neither of us is happy
> but neither of us wants to leave
> so we keep breaking one another
> and calling it love

Another of Kaur's identifiable devices is her "signing" of poems. The earliest example comes several pages into *Milk and Honey*, when a therapist asks "*how're you feeling*"; the poem concludes,

you pull the lump
in your throat out
with your teeth
and say *fine*
numb really

- midweek sessions

This initial instance of signing works like an especially literal title; the next section of text ("he was supposed to be / the first male love of your life / you still search for him / everywhere") ends with "*- father*", performing a similar function while adding a resemblance to the format of stage dialogue, while a subsequent part of this sequence ends, "*- to fathers with daughters*", adding a dedicatory function to the device.

Later, the caption-like titles become more conventionally imagistic or "literary", like when a long-ish prose poem signed "*- falsehood*" encapsulates and assigns a concept to its subject matter. Elsewhere, they add a voice that exists at a further remove, adding a lightly metatextual resonance: "the abused / and the / abuser // - *i have been both*". Subsequent signoffs include simplistic aphorisms that are in the imperative ("if the hurt comes / so will the happiness" is followed by "*- be patient*"). These signoffs function as both a conventionally stylized title as well as a conclusion that results from the brief poem to which it's appended, for instance, while at other points they describe the discursive form a given poem may resemble, blurring into the lines of the poem proper.

At once title, signature, and caption, the device appears to fumble with the idea of what a good title is, in the process gentling deconstructing the convention even as it becomes a more or less consistent part of the book's formatting. Also important to this dynamic is Kaur's use of the signoffs to summon conceptions of a mass, participatory readership. One short poem further into the book, in the section entitled "The Healing"—in its entirety, "perhaps the saddest of all / are those who live waiting / for someone they're not / sure exists"—ends "*- 7 billion people*". Shortly afterwards, this corny, global-scale summoning of a feeling of togetherness converts itself into a hailing of the universal individual. Signed "*- to all you young poets*", the poem reads in its first half:

your art
is not about how many people
like your work
your art
is about
if your heart likes your work
if your soul likes your work

and concludes, in the imperative, that the reader "must never / trade honesty / for relatability". The collection's final poem again refers to its own situation in the book format. It starts "you have made it to the end" and is signed "- *a love letter from me to you*". At this point the insistence on authenticity of voice begins to express itself in a way that evokes the homely print-culture format of the greeting card to hail a readership of poets with whom that format could reasonably be expected to resonate.

Moving forward from the earlier, especially fragmented poems, and the multivalent use of the signoff to sketch out these relationships, the book eases down onto the solid ground of confessional poetry, ending up at a quasi-teenaged or, in the context of the academy, sophomoric fixation on the honestly expressed. On a textual level, the blend of private sketchbook aesthetics, those resembling more the handwritten messages one intends to be read by a recipient, and recognizable print-book conventions folds Kaur's aesthetic into its ultimate existence as a saleable product—that is, an authentic book of poetry like one would find on the shelves of any real bookstore, suggesting again that one might look forward to one day having a book of one's own.

Kaur's ambiguous signing practice occurs again in the book's paratext, with explanatory sections signed "about the writer" and "about the book". The latter elucidates the themes and organization of the book using the same lineated proto-poetry of the book proper: "*milk and honey* is a / collection of poetry about / love / loss..."; "it is split into four chapters / each chapter serves a different purpose / deals with a different pain / heals a different heartache". These pages resemble a book-club list of discussion questions printed at the end of a popular trade edition, but without the obviously paratextual remove: what we're getting is more Kaur, tying things up for us just before we close the tangible book in front of us.

Just as the progression and form of the books represents a movement beyond social media, so has Kaur's career post-*Milk and Honey* continued this process. In a sense, it finds further culmination in her second book, *The Sun and Her Flowers* (2017), in which her evolving *Künstlerroman* comes to include quirky, funny, clever pieces that revel in the extent to which they have become real poems—ones that, if they could be separated from their bibliographic and authorial context, would be recognized as such even by Anglophone poetry's Rebecca Wattses. Take, especially, the following:

> even if they've been separated
> they'll end up together
> you can't keep lovers apart
> no matter how much
> i pluck and pull them
> my eyebrows always
> find their way
> back to each other
>
> - *unibrow*

The combination of irreverence and earnestness—the topic and joke of the signoff combined with the recognizable lyric craft of the line endings separated / together / apart, and the resonance of much / them, always / way—is key here. At points like this Kaur has come full circle from speaking-to-the-people rule-breaker back to the rarified practice of "real" poetry, with what might almost appear to Zapruder's befuddled students, in their confusion about what real meaning poetry might be hiding, as this kind of purposeful artifice. This half-wrought quality keeps the poem from being a completely "normal" poem—that is to say, a poem that is acceptedly literary or craft conscious. But it's also the thing that perhaps makes Kaur resonate with so many people. The original appeal remains in the irony and more mature versification, and the combination of the two is encapsulated in the signoff, now having evolved into something that, despite its placement at the end of the poem and following a hyphen, more obviously resembles a conventional title.

***

A few years out from her debut, Kaur's influence on poetry is palpable in a few ways. Most notably, her demonstrative, educative apparatus is being replicated in more specific areas—not the broad, general-public poetry sphere that Kaur's work seems to have summoned into existence as much as connected with, but rather a subculture in which a similarly educative dynamic obtains among younger writers with more uniform interests and goals.

John Barton has identified similarities between Kaur's poetry and that of Billy-Ray Belcourt (Driftpile Cree Nation), an author who has found popular appeal as well as success in Canadian literature's prize economy. Barton sees a doctrine of "NO FILTERS" in the work of both writers, lifting social-media language to describe the supposed lack of artifice in their poetry. Describing Belcourt's poems from *This Wound Is a World* (2017) as having "an impact so immediate they need only to be read once", Barton argues that Belcourt's seeming simplicity lucidly depicts the damages of settler colonialism and, in returning to family and culture, prevents his "academically gained intellectual apparatus" from becoming "mere theoretical badinage".

Belcourt's poetry often features an educative dynamic. Only instead of dealing in Kaur's universals—parental discord, substance abuse, intimacy—Belcourt constructs his emotive reflections using the tools of critical theory. Jumping ahead to *NDN Coping Mechanisms* (2019), one finds much of what Barton praises in Belcourt's debut:

> Poets pledge allegiance to a country I don't believe in.
> A country is how men hunt in the dark.
> A man I love but don't trust kisses me
> the way a soldier might press his face into the soil of his old country.

But the passage illustrates that simple sentiment and complex intellectualism are not exactly opposing parts in Belcourt's poetry. They are consciously co-occurring, as reflected in Belcourt's choice of placing "A Country Is How Men Hurt", a title that alone assumes knowledge of the anti-nationalist sentiment informing much literary study in Canada, up front. The language may seem impenetrable to someone who finds Kaur's work appealing but is armed only with a high-school or vocational-school diploma. By the end of an Honours BA, however, a discourse in which the settler-colonial state is conjured as a violent project of domination that masks the psychological deficits of those who enforce its boundaries practically rolls off the tongue, to educated people even functioning as a kind of shorthand for broader progressive values. To me, Belcourt's poems read like tightly stylized, at times almost impossibly compact versions of a graduate student's brainstorming session for a seminar paper.

This dynamic goes beyond the poetry's politics. At the book's midpoint, the poems take on more visual, ostensibly experimentalist forms. "Treaty 8" is an erasure poem that seems to be based on the titular document, the unequal treaty imposed in 1899 on the First Nations of the Lesser Slave Lake area of what is today central Alberta. Blocks of redacted text include within them revealed words and phrases. The first page of the poem, as rendered on my kindle reader, includes twenty-seven lines of prose, with a mere eighteen words surviving the redaction. What is pulled out of the first page of the text is the following passage: "THE LIMITS / OF // 1898 REPRESENTING // 1899 /// INDIAN / SUBJECTS / AND TO ARRANGE THEM WILL / THEM AND OTHER SUBJECTS / TO...." The poem is compelling on a visual level, its rows of textlessness radically physical in their simultaneous reproduction and destruction of a print document. Still, given that this document is already an explicitly political, administrative text, the erasure seems not to reveal anything deeper about that text as much as illustrate that one might use the erasure technique to highlight buried or insidious elements of such a document, any of which might hold within itself a poem for the enterprising poet-archivist. Existing alongside the important political and educative work the poem does is another iteration of "you can do it too"—but, significantly, in this case it's for the undergraduate or MA set as opposed to Kaur's larger and arguably more diverse social-media audience.

As Belcourt seems to be striking a chord with academically minded younger readers, Kaur's *Home Body* is following the mainstream media's appropriation of this language. In so doing, however, one gets the impression that she may be sacrificing

the wider appeal that made her persona and first two books
so notable. In much of *Home Body*, the imperative of the brief
signed poems is less affirming than preachy. I have a younger
normie cousin—someone who has not pursued a graduate degree
in the humanities—and while I'm not especially in touch with
her, I've noticed through her social media posts that she was
at some point interested in the Instapoetry genre. Whether that
included Kaur specifically, I don't know, but I can be reasonably
certain that a poem like the following—

> look for the women in the room
> who have less space than you
> listen
> hear them
> and act on what they're saying
>
> *- amplify indigenous. trans. black. brown. women of color voices.*

—is not quite as in keeping with her interests. The mainstreaming
of social-justice topics, along with the identity-based content
of her previous books, may mean that Kaur's readership will
remain intact. Even so, it's hard to imagine that moving further
into Belcourt's territory will widen her appeal. Belcourt is doing
deliberately political cultural work that foregrounds a set of
experiences and highlights historical and ongoing injustices. This
work, and engagement with it, highlights the myriad differences
of subject position, and, given this dynamic, I wonder whether
Belcourt would even desire fame like Kaur's. In moving closer to
this political emphasis on difference, Kaur might be undercutting
everything that made her work so appealing in the first place.

One finds similar contradictions in some recent iterations
of the importance-of-poetry genre of criticism. Burt, in *Don't
Read Poetry*, includes toward the beginning of Chapter Four the
following words: "This chapter shows how and why poets present
us with problems, why some poets choose to write poems that
do not make consistent sense, no matter how hard we work to
untangle them. It shows how opaque or resistant language can
instruct and delight, and how some non- or anti-sense in poetry
can help us spot nonsense, or hypocrisy, or lies, in the rest of
the world, outside poems". This strikes me as a disingenuous

oversimplification and mischaracterization, all under the guise of good intentions and education. No, this is not what "nonsense" does in a poem, as a Harvard professor who is familiar with $L=A=N=G=U=A=G=E$ and everything that came after surely understands. Still more frustratingly, the introduction to this paragraph anti-sensically ends: "And I'll end with a poet not normally considered avant-garde or ultradifficult, and a poem that sums up several of the reasons that difficulty can give some poems not only an irreplaceable energy but also a way to resist bad ideas and bad societies, hence a reason to exist".

Bad ideas and bad societies? I wonder if Burt would be willing to declare anything but a rally of Trump supporters (or video-game Nazis) as the latter. With no sign that the average (working-class) person will ever improve their situation under neoliberalism or whatever crueler derivative of it emerges following the pandemic, all the young-ish reader can hope for is to be a success story—to become famous. With progressives—politicians as well as culture technicians—having failed to present anything like an appealing worldview or a way forward (beyond getting social-media likes for shaming a small range of "bad people and bad societies" with sufficient vigour), it is perhaps heartening that, as Kaur shows us, a new generation of readers have come to envision the heartening as synonymous with the heartfelt. But it's a shame that this chapter will have to end by asking if the appeal of Kaur's *you could do it too* may resonate as *you too can be someone*—a destination that, for younger people of most backgrounds, seems increasingly out of reach

Part 2
EN GARDE: CONTESTING FORM, EXPERIMENT, AND MUSIC

On Formalism

In *Subverting the Lyric* (2008), rob mclennan argues for the importance of process- over results-based writing. As part of this position, he makes a loaded claim about the two "sides" that supposedly emerge in relation to this debate: one being those with "a more conservative poetic" and the other a "nebulous" formation consisting of writers who are "quite content simply to ignore the whole business" of what mclennan characterizes as the "potshots" coming from conservative reviews and essays. mclennan employs some degree of ironic distance, implying that he isn't quite validating this antagonism. Still, the innocence he attributes to this wide swath of process-oriented do-gooders raises some interesting questions. The so-called "conservatives" in the equation—by which he might mean people like Carmine Starnino, Jason Guriel, and Zachariah Wells, or just those whose poetry includes a preoccupation with line-by-line sonic detail and whose critical writing espouses a privileging of craft, almost always on the level of the single, well-wrought lyric poem— don't seem to care about mclennan's conception of poetry as peacefully exploring and easing into its existence on the page. They are the brutal standard-bearers who demand a certain kind of result rather than the free play and open-mindedness required for the more serious, or at least more sociable, poetry devotee. The latter attitude may just be a symptom of wanting to seem kind: who wouldn't prefer gentle declarations about the dangers of not letting poems speak for themselves over a brutally negative review? If we take the division seriously, on the other hand, we might wonder what a worthwhile poem even looks like, or, by extension, whether anything at all we call a poem is equally valuable. If this is the case, how do these nebulous, content, nice people themselves decide when something they write or read is or isn't compelling, or effective, or anything at all?

A similar, but more focused and more militant, objection to the idea of universally recognizable standards comes from a camp that seems quite interested in enforcing standards of its own. The Kootenay School of Writing, which, according to Clint Burnham in *The Only Poetry That Matters: Reading the Kootenay School of Writing* (2011), inhabits a different poetic universe entirely by continuing Language writing's engagement with the materiality of the signifier in a context that foregrounds "a political economy of counter-traditions, of marginalized spaces and bodies in the history of Vancouver". I find Burnham's conception of this praxis—of a poetry that exists not only in its texts but in the daily practices of its participants—appealing, but for reasons other than the generative and participatory work of poetry I argue for here. (That is, I see precisely this dynamic animating poetries and poetry cultures more generally.) Burnham's claims that the KSW's collage-based poetics is disjunctive syntactically as well as socially—that it uses the very substance of language for both representing and performing an alternative politics, and from this standpoint is able to address "the master *qua* master-signifier, and also the master as power itself"[1]—is premised on the group in question being somehow more valid than those emerging in the multivalent practice of contemporary poetry, which itself has internalized and reiterated in various forms the

---

1   Burnham accounts for the fact that such poets are working from within the realities of institutions, arguing that the KSW "also takes on the power structures of the university, assuming the trappings not just of institutional power but also the jargon of inauthenticity that characterizes the syntax and vocabulary of post-modernism." Still, the singularity of the group and context, which I'll discuss further in the two essays on the avant-garde, suggests that his demarcation leaves out writing that does much of the same work he claims only the KSW can.

lessons of poststructuralism and Language poetry from which the KSW pushed off.[2]

Burnham's case may be deliberately provocative and over-assured, but its value lies in part that he too regards poets or categories of poet as firmly located in their own incomparable circumstances. My point, though, is that he looks at the one group as they exist on a landscape that, at least by now, is more flattened than his take lets on. There's a myopia like what one finds in demonizations of the results-focused group: both conceptions of an ostensibly superior subsection of contemporary poetry strike me as either wrongheaded or disingenuous because these groups are delimited not by the poetry as much as by how its advocates describe their own work, or just by where they're located socially. And, more crucially when it comes to the poetry itself, feel-good talk about letting the poems exist free of any expectation denies the validity of the work behind them, at least if we attempt to systematize this brand of open-mindedness to cover its results as they actually exist on a page. Pretty much any poetry worth reading and speaking of is doing exactly what an attention to process permits: we should of course regard any poem as singular, but also as existing in whatever messy, shared landscape is created as a result of these varied practices. Poetry exists in a capacious area where formalism is itself a process, and where foregrounding an appreciation of process is itself a kind of codified writing that might be described as formalism. And, as I've suggested in "Reviewing Reviewing", regarding poetry in this way means that it's impossible to conceive of even a minimum of agreed-upon standards that allow even comparative, let alone evaluative, criticism of individual volumes.

I very much want to be on the side of process. My problem is that I think doing so creates a false dichotomy. If caring about

---

2   Brian M. Reed's *Nobody's Business: Twenty-First Century Avant-Garde Poetics* (2013) treats the replacement of an experimental-traditional divide in contemporary US poetry by a so-called "hybrid poetics" as widely accepted. His description of this process as entailing the mainstream acceptance of many of the techniques of Language Poetry is astute, but his counterargument that the US poetry avant-garde lives on in work that critiques "language and literary form in the context of class struggle that aspires to bring readers to a consciousness of their place in that conflict" is eerily similar to subjective defences like Burnham's.

the end product of one's poetry writing is bad, where does that really get us? Back, perhaps, to the idea that any poem written just five minutes ago is not only valid but, at the risk of following slippery-slope logic, in fact more interesting and authentic in its spontaneity than are the uninnovative products of a veteran lyricist's labours. The sentiment—and I realize I'm presenting a simplified version of a series of more or less nuanced objections— is born of good intentions, maybe. But valorizing process-based writing above all else, as does a hardened relativist critic I'll discuss shortly, is at bottom a form of corruption: it equates value with the circumstances of a poem's production, which are usually linked inextricably with who we are, where we are, whom we know, and whether the set of experiences we're hashing out in an anything-goes format is considered by insiders as experience that is in need of amplification. The more we valorize daily facts and the act of writing in real time and space, the less the words that are written enter the equation. I think this is true no matter how fusty we might find the notion of a well-wrought poem that is widely (or, gasp, universally) recognizable as such.

I use the term formalism cautiously. Although it's fraught with historical baggage, it continues to be a useful term in discussions of Canadian poetry. One reason for this is the influence of Carmine Starnino, whose tastes were summarized and somewhat systematized in his introduction to *The New Canon: An Anthology of Canadian Poetry* (2005). Taking issue with the lazy free-verse poetics he saw as defining contemporary Canadian poetry— "the plain, the soft-spoken, the flatly prosy, the paraphrasingly simple, the accessibly Canadian"—Starnino used his anthology to highlight instead two forces he claimed were regarded as attacking the status quo: experimental poets and those who he saw being demonized as "capital-F formalists", or formalists "prefixed with 'neo' to convey the drasticness of their suspected conservatism". Starnino challenged derogatory characterizations of the latter group, instead introducing what he saw as a loosely allied number of poets whose distaste for "the prose-domesticated mainstream" produced the work populating his anthology.

Including work by writers as diverse as Ken Babstock, Stephanie Bolster, George Elliott Clarke, Anita Lahey, David

McGimpsey, and Karen Solie, Starnino's anthology highlights poems that eschew plainspoken, Purdy-esque free verse in favour of sonically colourful, metrically tight patterning. The introduction often describes this sonic complexity in vivid and yet ultimately subjective terms: "pounded-on spontaneity", for instance, or "aggressive musicality". What seems to be at work in many of the poems included is a foregrounded interplay of sound and content, often occurring on the level of the individual line.

All of which is to say that *The New Canon* showcases a painstakingly crafted poetics that is nonetheless recognizable as well-wrought poetry—its conception of innovation includes a skilled use of poetic devices that will be recognizable as such to anyone who has studied the form in any detail, including using tried-and-tested handbooks such as M.H. Abrams' *Glossary of Literary Terms*. Starnino presents an intuitive poetics that, because of its incremental building on notions of tradition, has at times been streamlined or simplified into universal ideas of skill and quality. One such equation of poetics and quality comes from Jason Guriel, in the years following the publication of *The New Canon* an active and well-regarded (but also controversial) poetry critic. Guriel stated clearly in a review of Eric Ormsby's *Time's Covenant: Selected Poems* (2007) that "a poem's primary responsibility is to be excellent". Between the subjective nature of Starnino's description of such a poetics, the very loosely affiliated nature of the poets included in *The New Canon*, and—crucially—the explicitly oppositional nature of the non-movement, however, one could be forgiven for mistaking this kind of quasi-formalism as itself a processual poetics.

Nevertheless, explicit rejections of this supposedly monolithic entity abound. Perhaps the most extreme rebuff of this poetics—or, perhaps, caricature of it—comes as part of Donato Mancini's *You Must Work Harder to Write Poetry of Excellence: Crafts Discourse and the Common Reader in Canadian Poetry Book Reviews* (2012), a book that, while ostensibly about the act of book reviewing and attendant ideas of writerly authority, is also a loud slap in the face for those who think in terms of craft. Mancini argues that a "consensus on literary value" that ignores or rejects the fact that "hundreds of Canadian poets have risen from bed each day self-tasked only to conspire against the values of official verse culture" continues to hold sway in Canadian literary culture. According to Mancini, this supposedly dominant view of poetry is enforced by a mode of criticism that prizes emotional intelligibility and identifiable, often quaintly nationalist messages; these in turn are presented as "natural, concrete components of (what was once called) quality". Adjudicative reviewing, directed at the fantasy of a Common Reader who can "set the terms of aesthetic morality" and "prescribe (often retroactively) which compositional practices are licit", constructs the conception of craft—itself informed by conceptions of middle-class "productive activity" that might be a successor to a reputable professional career—as the factor that limits the range of Canadian verse.

Craft—I have my own issues with the word. I agree with Mancini that craft as work seems at times to recreate ideas of middle-class comfort in which the tropes of manual labour are honourably approximated and repurposed. But, as the arguments I'm making in these pages might suggest, what I'm not going to take issue with is more slippery and multivalent ideas of effort. As a review of the book by Andrea Bennett pointed out, Mancini's deconstruction of what were then already recognized as problematic reviewing tropes, combined with his few mentions of ostensibly more nuanced postmodern reviewing practices, erects an "equivalent (and similarly ideologically blind) moral high ground for the avant-garde". Mancini relentlessly dismantles these subjects to the extent that there's not much one couldn't fold into his nebulous group of targets. Take, for example, his opening caricature of the values underpinning a 1961 review by J.R. Colombo: "Real poets write real poetry. Real poetry is good poetry. Which poetry is good? The poetry in the good (= big budget) magazines. Quality is legible: Read it". The passage sort of works as a poem in itself, which is ironic given that his anti-everything edgelordery also implicitly takes down anything like writing, engagement, thinking or, I guess, even editing a text to the extent that the clipped phrases of his caricature must have been. If hard work is bad, and if all we can really expect from any text is the radical particularity uncovered by a postmodernist set of values that views art objects as fundamentally incomparable, then what keeps every single one of us from scrawling down whatever comes to mind and calling it a radically processual snapshot of an incomparably singular self that can't possibly be held up to anything as debased as evaluation?

I suppose there are a few answers. Critics like Mancini might disingenuously claim that a revolutionary utopia would let us do just this. Keeping to his reasoning in a more strictly logical way, one might find that there's no there there in poetry—that it's ultimately nothing more than its politics. If we're all radical particularities, as he claims, then oppressed or hitherto unheard voices are the only ones that matter, making poetry a politics less of the utterance than of a right to representation. Practically, Mancini, whom I've never met, probably believes a little bit of this while also believing that he and his friends just happen to have voices that are worth hearing (and, therefore, that the rest of us should be content with our notebooks).

A snide book-length argument like Mancini's, full of snobbish insults as it is, warrants the mildly personal redress I'm offering. But I'll move on in favour of making a more generative case for the value of what some have insistently but perhaps *narrowly* called "craft". I say narrowly because my own concept of the word includes the sense of time and attention paid to both craft as adept composition within established limits as well as the creative engagement required to produce work that is to some extent recognizable within these limits as well as unrecognizable in its pathbreaking elements (or, at least, the originality of its permutation of more recognizable techniques). This kind of careful engagement is, I think, what is often meant by commonly occurring judgements of a poem's "quality", even if these judgements are regarded as universalizing in their values or limited in their recognition of what constitutes poetry that is worth our time. To demonstrate how there is always an interplay of form and process, I'll discuss here two seemingly different poets whose work, despite displaying various experimental characteristics, is nevertheless well-wrought in a recognizable sense. Not in a way that invites suspicion as to some conservatism that lurks inside the poetics of either, but rather by evoking attention, effort, and care. And, in the process, interrogating what is recognizable as poetry and how far into the unknown—and into one another—those identifiable qualities can extend.

Helen Hajnoczky, a Calgary-based poet and visual artist who has published poetry collections with then-Montreal based Snare Books and Toronto's Coach House, effortlessly crosses boundaries between process-based or experimental poetry and verse that draws on more conventional devices. In *Magyarázni* (2016), she adds visual poetry to the mix: the book consists of a series of dual poems—one visual and one written in conventional, even somewhat neoformalist verse—for each letter of the Hungarian alphabet. One of my favourite of Hajnoczky's poems, "Cserkészek" plays with the sonic overlaps between Hungarian and English words, phrases, and orthography, invoking along the way chance etymological resonances between the two languages. The sounds of its Hungarian title are spread among English lines while echoing, expanding, contradicting, or otherwise compromising the meaning of the Hungarian term: "Check if you're ready / Roll and tighten your neckerchief / Roll on your stockings, stand at attention".

But the formal play doesn't stand apart from the subject matter. "Cserkészek" depicts the process by which individuals—perhaps here resonating as well with the avant trope of the hopelessly outdated, lyricizing poet—are socialized into something like a collective that is animated by more abstract beliefs:

> Deliver your lines with conviction
> A more personable person
> A more magyar Hungarian
>
> Paint eggs, throw rosewater
> Thread needles, weave leather
> Serve dinner to your elders[.]

The first of these two stanzas makes chiasmus out of two languages, "A more personable person" linking and juxtaposing surface-level affability with raw personhood, while the following line echoes and flips the arrangement, using "magyar"—the autonym for *Hungarian*—to modify the English-language demonym. In the next, folk practices are expressed using similarly blurring consonance, assonance, and pacing.

The allusion to the nineteenth-century "national awakenings" of East-Central Europe uses the image of a series of standardized national subjects to expose the conceptions of uniqueness, personability, and maturity from which conceptions of a responsible self tend to be constructed in developed, individualistic societies. And yet the dynamic also resonates with Hajnoczky's inhabitation of both avant and lyric worlds. Just as the poem's concrete engagement with the sounds of its Hungarian title works in the spirit of Language writing's attention to the materiality of the words and sounds themselves, so does this poetics articulate the arrangement of idiosyncrasies and incomparabilities that must nevertheless produce the lyric voice's "personable person".[3] The point is that her tight formal patterning and attention to detail don't mark Hajnoczky's work as dated or backward looking; they're still further from features that mark her as giving in to the masculinized and class-stratified structure determining poetic value. Rather, the "craft" of the poems is in the stitches holding together the multiple modes (free verse, prose, visual poetry, limitedly referential repetitiousness) and constituting them as recognizable for readerships familiar with any of them. The visual pieces accompanying the poems could be regarded as in the lineage of the avant-garde as opposed to something that can coexist easily with what might be denigrated as simply lyric poetry. But what sets Hajnoczky apart is the detailed, multivalent traditionalism—encompassing folk art, lyric, historically identifiable variants of (at least at the time) experimental poetry—that holds the various modes together.

While *Magyarázni*, published by Coach House Books, is striking in its trade-publication elegance, Hajnoczky has gone in different directions following its appearance. In February 2017 she published a chapbook called *No Right on Red* with rob

---

3   This reading of the poem follows the one that appears in *Oblique Identity: Form and Whiteness in Recent Canadian Poetry* (Frog Hollow, 2019) where I took Hajnoczky's imagery to stand for the singularity harmfully implied by many conceptions of whiteness more than as a comment on the ostensible divisions between lyric and avant-garde poetry.

mclennan's above/ground press. Consisting of an unbroken six-page swath of prose, *No Right on Red* reiterates a cliched Anglophone experience of Montreal in which the city is a stop-off in a coming-of-age story but, inevitably, not a place one can remain. With its title and its final sentence—"We are waiting at a red light to turn right"—it repeats a lowbrow Anglo-Canadian joke about Montreal's traffic laws. But Hajnoczky's prose does something similar to her poetry, stitching common experiences together using fleeting almost-repetitions that recall Gertrude Stein. On the final page—

> We are trying to memorize the way the church spires and walk-ups look in the rain. We are trying to remember the way the water trickled from the ceiling of the metro, the way Pall Malls smell, the taste of Labatt 50. We are saying our last goodbye here, now we're the ones leaving. We are remembering the stone and green and ache of this city.

—polyptoton ("memorize" and "remember") melts into "metro" and then "Pall Malls smell", with the reference to Labatt 50 blending low Anglo culture and French names. The "last goodbye", coming before one more "remembering", is stretched and echoed in the "green and ache of this city", the result being that a recognizable privileged-student story is at once rendered as real experience and yet, due to its formalism foregrounded as fictional, as if the embroidery gives us as much tackiness as tactility.

Hajnoczky's movements toward prose as well as toward smaller formats published with her own ?! Press continue her navigations beyond any dichotomy of form and formlessness. This movement toward a handmade, almost arts-and-crafts aesthetic puts a new spin on what Kaplan Harris has identified (in a quasi-review of Charles Bernstein's *All the Whiskey in Heaven: Selected Poems*) as the "bibliographic map" or "zine ecology" that becomes visible when we attend to the way particular poems resonate with paratextual features of the small-press formats in which they appeared. Harris describes, for instance, how one of Bernstein's cut-up poems resonates with the cover image of the sixteenth issue of San Francisco zine *Tottel*'s. The smallest-of-the-small solo offerings that include this recent run of Hajnoczky's poems, however, reduce this kind of collaborative, social, and temporal resonance into a more personal, literally handcrafted immediacy. *Other Observations* is wound a little less tightly than some of Hajnoczky's poems, its sonic resonances spread over an almost picaresque doggerel. Beginning,

> A flimsy crutch to hold the light
> Day's back strained against the night
> We stroll in sunset's consumptive rattle.
> He scuttles me through muffled streets
> Our tedious retreats

it spools out into a series of false beginnings, with subsequent sections beginning, for example, "And yes again, and yet again / I plan to leave and plan to leave / But again I turn back and take my keys" and "And the evening, the night, turn so sleeplessly! / Churned by restless feet, / Raw ... exhausted ... indiscrete, / Spread across our bed, heavy with humidity". The series of microchapbooks released around this time incorporate the visual-art elements throughout, while Hajnoczky's prose-formalist skills are given room to breathe in an at once complete and yet self-contained form. *Other Observations,* according to its acknowledgements published in "an unfinished version" by No Press in 2010 and subsequently, in its "complete" form, in May 2015 at *Dusie*, rob mclennan's blog of Tuesday poems, and in *The Calgary Renaissance* (Chaudiere Books, 2016), in being presented once again in a handmade format separate from those publications, smooths out the textual and contextual details that make up Harris' ecology. It turns us instead to the multiplicity of formal characteristics that nevertheless combine as recognizable elements in Hajnoczky's evolving style.

variations on the stillness of motion, published in a numbered edition of twenty, also integrates its format with a broader, animating formalism. Consisting of seventeen watercolour paintings, each of which is reproduced on the facing page with a handwritten poem on tracing paper layered over it, Hajnockzy's prose-centric poetry is especially tightly coiled, its formal play resembling the unpunctuated, run-on sentences frequently used by younger social-media users. The first poem, written seemingly without line breaks, or line breaks that are forced by the constraint of the watercolour inset's size as well as the self-imposed six-line constraint governing the poems,[4] reads, "forgiven forgoes a process / we are forgiveness when we / pick apart a forgotten part / of giving our harness or it / pulls the getting of forment / this is important". With the next one, Hajnoczky reproduces *Magyarázni*'s use of sonic shifts to determine content, with the "forgive" root mutating into "we pour the firmament in since / there's a cement in movement...." The ostensible formalism isn't a conscious throwback (and it's certainly not an unfortunate register that jars with directions she goes in that are commonly associated with formal innovation or progressive values). On the contrary, it's the thing that holds it all together amid the experiments and small-scale production and distribution. It's at once the heart of the matter, as Starnino insists, but not (as his contentious takes often imply) in that it's a genre or mode of poetry. And it's precisely this kind of technique, pulsing through an evolving style and varied approaches and engagements, that makes Mancini's argument that any notion of quality or agreed-upon standards is oppressive seem like little more than contrarianism. If putting work into poetry is somehow suspect, or fascist, then what, exactly, is the radically particular ideal? What does it actually look like? Not putting in any effort at all? Being naturally a genius, that hopelessly outdated masculinist romantic trope? Being outwardly, unsettlingly political? Or just knowing the right people? In contemporary poetry, perhaps supplanting what is now Formerly Official Verse Culture, this kind of haphazardly, socially defined political orientation is the new Official Verse Culture.

Very different from Hajnoczky's trajectory is the body of work produced by Moez Surani. I first encountered Surani's work when I was a PhD student in Kingston, and I saw him read some romantic lyric poems about (among other topics) visiting statues of Buddha while he was teaching English in South Korea. At that point the author of two collections and a few chapbooks of decidedly lyric

---

4   See Hajnoczky's website, https://www.ateacozyisasometimes.com/chapbooks#/variations-on-the-stillness-of-motion-1/, for a description of the chapbook and its format.

poetry,[5] what Surani did next would be a departure from those poems about an aimless year abroad. The 184 pages of 2016's *Operations* (or عملية *Operación Opération Operation* 行动 *Операция*), published by Toronto's Book*hug Press and described on its back-cover copy as the work of a "poet-provocateur", consists mainly of a list of military operations carried out by United Nations member states between 1945 and 2006, organized chronologically by year.

I was initially skeptical of what seemed to me an abrupt change in direction for Surani. But, reading Operations, I didn't get the impression that the book was just an opportunistic realignment of poetic sensibility. Despite protestations (or approving claims) that conceptual writing ought not to be read in a traditional, page by page sense of the term, the contents of Surani's list can indeed be read productively, and with enjoyment. The cumulative effect of listing the operation names makes the reader register the violence of an international order held together by competing hegemons and, at least until very recently, the United States alone. What's more, swaths of the list are downright funny. Take, for instance,

    Dazzlem (1967-1968)
    Blue Max
    Banish Beach
    Night Bolt

and

    Toan Thang [Complete Victory]
    Burlington Trail
    Norfolk Victory
    Jasper Square
    Inferno
    Scrotum II
    Velvet Hammer
    Clifton Corral
    Duck Blind[.]

---

5   Surani's previous trade collections are *Reticent Bodies* (2009) and *Floating Life* (2012), both with Wolsak and Wynn; his chapbooks published before 2016 included the small-press offerings *The Viscount's Goats* (2004) and *Cairo* (2009).

In addition to the fact that these passages sound more like the discographies of Hair Metal bands than lists of names conforming to Winston Churchill's statement (referred to in Surani's introduction) that such missions "ought not to be described by code words which imply a boastful or overconfident sentiment", they can be read in a surprisingly traditional literary-critical way as expressive of US foreign policy's descent into irresponsible machismo and Western popular culture's reflection of this situation in mass-culture genres like action movies and theatrical hard rock. Strangely, Surani's shift to the supposedly non-referential has made for better poetry than much of what one finds in the pages of his first two books.

The next time I saw Surani read, as part of the Lit Live Reading Series at Hamilton's Staircase Theatre in November 2018, he spoke of a collaborative project with cross-disciplinary artist Nina Leo entitled *Heresies*, in which the pair commissioned scents associated with cities whose names carry markedly political resonances. One of these "olfactory poems" ("The Chat") represented Baghdad, and Surani spoke with relish of the exhaust fumes that were an especially notable aspect of the scent named for the city that was at that point suffering under the years-long ISIL insurgency. Which is to say that no one can accuse Surani of having smoothed out the excesses of his artistic practice. All the more impressive, then, is that Surani's next book of poems, *Are the Rivers in Your Poems Real?* (2019), doesn't quite synthesize these aspects of his previous output but somehow sits atop the romanticism and excess and self-assuredness while still evoking the provocative elements of *Operations*.

The book uses the maximal, information-saturated outlook of *Operations* to generate a formalist probing of the natural world in its concrete reality and necessarily abstract aspects (how does one conceive of a "natural world", after all, without relying on the limited vistas with which we have experience?). Jonathan Ball, in a review in the *Winnipeg Free Press*, refers to Surani as a conceptual writer even as he acknowledges that the poet "doesn't always work in this mode"; his review focuses on "The Backburner", a conceptual piece in the book, acknowledging that Surani's poems "work hard to interrogate themselves even as they interrogate you". Nick Thran also comments on this bifurcation of modes in Surani's work, describing *Are the Rivers in Your Poems Real?* as "a book of lyric and conceptual inventories and travelogues". He finds the lyric register featuring speakers that are "often situated upon or in proxy to the very real rivers of the world", with the poems in this mode highlighting desires "to be known, to be seen, to be understood and to be loved". Thran regards the conceptual approach, on the other hand, as being comprised of "stricter, more rational and visual concepts of world citizenship, highlighting the various vectors of power, which have the capacity to dwarf the individual and their desires". I want to argue here that, while the two modes in the book conform with such a distinction, the eponymous poem with which the collection opens bridges the lyric-conceptual binary that, at first glance, may seem to apply to Surani's recent work, and that its craft or formalism is one of the ways in which it does so.

The poem begins with images of an already sullied natural world ("Do they eddy and whirl concaves into rocks, / mingle with plastic bags, effluents, rags, / rose petals in their rush?"), distant history ("It is unbelievable to me that Lithuania was once huge"), and references to the Zodiac and Christ. These unfold as part of a series of questions that begins with the poem's (and book's) title and eventually become rhetorical. But is that central question actually rhetorical? How might one answer? Literally—"I am writing about real rivers"? Or is it getting at the problem of writing as strictly representation—not a "real" thing, in which case the rivers are of course not real insofar as the text generates images in the reader's mind. What's more, the questions don't seem to be invested enough in their own terms really to function as such. As for "your", it's also an apostrophe, perhaps? But who is the speaker querying? Regardless, it's a lyric poem in the form of a conversation. And the question repeats and changes, with "Are the rivers in your poems like the course of archetypal romance?" coming just before the characters from *Wuthering Heights* make an appearance: "Didn't Emily have Heathcliff's oriental love / tear like a brutal river through Catherine?". Which is to say that it now seems like he is talking about writing, including genres of writing, with "romance" signifying perhaps romanticism but also romance in the sense of a story that is comfortable within a universe of known values.

Then we have another iteration of the question—"Do your rivers exist before and after the duration of your poems?"—that asks whether writing can succeed in representing, or perhaps preserving, "real" things, in any sense at all and for how long. The line "the elements pouring through you and your interpretative mind" seems like it might use the figure of zeugma, with the duality of water literally ingested and also metaphorically flowing as thought process. But the physical "you" and metaphorical nature of "your" are, after all, intertwined. Are the senses in which "pouring" is used really so different? Perhaps Surani is playing with the zeugma, asking to what extent the device's various levels of meaning can really be regarded as distinct, or at least what value there is in doing so. These swaths of the poem employ conventional poetic devices so that their multiple valences draw attention to the seams in the semic and lexical representations that are the fabric of lyric poetry.

Many of the very sonic emphases and syntactical patterns that define Starnino's supposedly conservative method of writing and reading poetry, as they appear in Surani's poem, draw attention to themselves and question the basic representative function. It's a poem laid bare in a way that approximates the re-presentation and defamiliarization of material things that is at the heart of the conceptualism that critics like Ball and Thran present as separate from Surani's lyric poetry. Surani's long lines and prosaic syntax coexist with the formal qualities that mark the poem, reflecting the ongoing conversation. He also provides lists—examples not always of zeugma but more frequently parallel elements. These representations of the abundance of the world play with the rhetorical question of the poem's title, in the process foregrounding poetry as a conversation about problems— of authorship, of representation, of "realness"—we should keep talking about. By extension, our relationship with the world (natural and geopolitical, as in the line "A city suburb? A field of / oil seeds or sugarcane?") must also be relentlessly questioned.

The sum of it all seems to be a multivalent questioning of the world around us and our role in it—something that sounds a lot like the purportedly radical qualities of certain experimentally oriented categories. But this happens precisely as a result of the conventional lyric characteristics of the poem. The final image could add to this reading, or it could undermine it—he's sad that he, in questioning, "cannot be perfect" for the world. The formally energized yet also streamlined characteristics stylize and disperse the poem's lyric interrogation to the extent that it carries out a conceptual re-presentation of itself even while unfolding as an ostensibly traditionalist lyric text. In "Are the Rivers in Your Poems Real?", the authorial manipulation that defines so-called formalism undermines the idea that craft is conservative. It also, like the other poems in this essay, reminds us of the inutility of experimental-mainstream binaries as well as the looser distinctions between process- and product-oriented writing that have persisted in approximating them. Since the formation, persistence, and falling away of such demarcations is itself both process and discursive product—for some, seemingly, the stuff that comprises one's entire aesthetic or poetic worldview—these binaries might be as messily relevant as they are ultimately meaningless. This kind of trap is set throughout the woods of contemporary poetry—including in the next essay.

Whose Solitudes? Reconsidering
Sina Queyras and Carmine Starnino

Montreal has persisted as something like a bastion of both experimental and traditionalist English-language poetry, with card-carrying members of the former, such as Sina Queyras and Darren Wershler, sharing space with David Solway and Carmine Starnino, champions of convention. Of course, more interesting (and accurate) than Montreal's famously dual demography is its multiple facets and fragments, as well as its singular demography. That both poetry camps are equally at home there doesn't seem especially remarkable. Reconsidering a notorious(ly) Montreal rivalry from the past few years might, however, indicate a different kind of multiplicity and indeterminacy flowing through the place's poetics: a shifting that's visible also in the gradual, ongoing replacement in English-language North American poetry of experimental-traditional binaries by those based on political engagement but also, maybe, in the at once surface-level and entirely real vicissitudes of personality, reputation, and attitude. It's a mixture that might be apprehended as a lingering duality but that, like the city's ostensible bilingualism, is a more fluid entity, comprised of processes of shapeshifting and exchange that are as mutable as they are socially and practically significant.

To provide some larger context, one might identify as a possible turning point in this regard the 2015 Goldsmith affair— that is, when Kenneth Goldsmith read "The Body of Michael Brown", a poem comprised solely of the recently murdered

Brown's autopsy report. Subsequently, Cathy Park Hong claimed in *The New Republic* that Goldsmith's conceptualism was being eclipsed by "a new movement in American poetry" that was "galvanized by the activism of Black Lives Matter" and "spearheaded by writers of color"; Park Hong saw these new activist poets as alternately "redefining the avant-garde" or "fueling a raw politics into the personal lyric". Also in 2015, Joshua Clover's "The Genealogical Avant-Garde", published in *Lana Turner Journal*, condemned an avant-garde that is self-satisfied and affirmative, calling instead for the establishment of an avant-garde that is "newly historical", "negationist", and attuned to "lived social antagonism". Considering such developments, it seems that North American poetry is in a process of inscribing a new binary that puts explicitly progressive politics at odds with apolitical poetry of a vast range of forms. The result is that figures like Goldsmith and Christian Bök—Wershler's co-conspirators in the development of conceptual writing—at times resemble Starnino's apolitical traditionalism (or at least a traditional experimentalism) as much as they do the social progressivism defining many avant-gardists.

To test this hypothesis, I'll contrast Queyras' "Endless Inter-States" (from 2005's *Expressway*) with Starnino's "San Pellegrino" (from 2016's *Leviathan*). Looking at these two poems—not as iterations of their respective authors' poetics or personas but as similarly lyric, somewhat narratively oriented texts that nevertheless command formal features in a way that marks them as craft-conscious poetry—shows not only that each poem adheres to "traditional" formal conventions, but also that political orientation is the most notable difference between the two. "Endless Inter-States" resists traditional gender roles and their part in maintaining systems of oppression (upholding such roles only insofar as they are useful as reference points in a process of revision and self-creation), and "San Pellegrino" works within such constructions (its critique of them contained within coming-of-age tropes and growing knowledge of the firmly located self).

Queyras herself has, in the essay "Lyric Conceptualism, a Manifesto in Progress" destabilized oppositions between the two poetic modes—including in the first part of the essay's title. She regards the Lyric Conceptualist as having "moved beyond the digestible and the unreadable", instead embracing a conceptually informed experimental poetics that, rather than presenting existing texts in original or abstract forms, "does not accept that content does not matter" and yet "still appreciates the way that content does not always matter". Notably, Queyras' enlarged conceptualism puts forward a tripartite division of contemporary poetics that roughly correlates to a model Starnino has put forward:

> Many conceptual poets are models for Lyric Conceptualism.
>
> Many Language poets are models for Lyric Conceptualism.
>
> Many lyric poets are models for Lyric Conceptualism.
>
> Lyric Conceptualism, then, is not new.

Starnino's introduction to *The New Canon* denigrates what he regards as the typical free-verse (i.e. lyric) of later twentieth-century Canadian poetry. Presumably, what Queyras refers to as conceptual poets would be included in Starnino's conception of experimental or avant-garde poets. Meaning that, if we can regard Queyras' preferred, or suggested, mode of lyric conceptualism as analogous to the dynamic, formally alert poetry with which Starnino fills his anthology, the third option in their existing poetic universes would be alternatively Language poets (for Queyras) and those earlier, unfashionably traditionalist lyricists, or "capital-F formalists", Starnino regards as unfairly maligned.

So, while it may be difficult to think of two poets who are commonly regarded as so diametrically opposed as Queyras and Starnino, their own manifestos reveal some degree of overlap. Where Starnino regards himself and his chosen poetics as succeeding previous notions of verse that is markedly structured, Queyras envisions a lyric conceptualism that takes cues from her own third term (Language poetry) as much as the free verse and experimental traditions Starnino rejects. Queyras is (at least insofar as she positions her own poetics) expansive where Starnino is combative—and the maintenance of these distinctions is likely conscious to some degree. Despite the difference in stance, the two in fact share a similarly oriented conception of recent North American poetics.

It's probably in part due to this difference in attitude that Queyras is regularly extolled in progressive poetry communities, the academic world, and the Twitterverse as one of Canada's foremost innovative poets and feminist thinkers. Numerous articles exist on her transformative uses of online platforms (initially blogging and later Twitter), as well as the immediacy of her 2006 poetry collection *Lemon Hound* in particular. Suzanne Zelazo writes, for instance, that the books fulfills her previous works' "echo[ing] a history of women's writing from and of the margins" in that, for the first time, "the poet's use of form merges seamlessly with her content, depicting the perfect liminality of Gilles Deleuze and Félix Guattari's 'becoming-woman'", therefore "troubling normative conceptions of influence and development, artistically as well as psycho-socially", in this way demonstrating the idea that such categories are permanently contested and in flux. Heather Milne, meanwhile, argues that *Lemon Hound* problematizes as well "the humanist subject and its dualisms of nature/culture, human/animal, and human/machine".

Starnino is seldom praised in this way; his accomplishments can perhaps best be measured not with such scholarly assessments but rather with the outrage of literary critics and progressive readerships. His spirited reviews and editorial work, both perhaps best embodied in his introduction to the anthology *The New Canon*, often rely on subjective notions of taste, while comments such as his dismissal of the importance of CWILA's annual count make the man (more than his poetry) a frequent topic of criticism. Even the few extant academic engagements with Starnino's work seem caught in this gravitational pull; Katye Seip has argued that Starnino's poetry creates an "'anti-exile,' audience driven, communicative aesthetic". The subsequent outline of Seip's argument seems explicitly to corral Starnino's critical and journalistic salvos and then find them in his poetry itself; she lists Starnino's "using the technique of direct address", "encouraging reader participation through interactive poetic genres such as the riddle poem", and attempting "to be precise in his use of language with the aim of making his poetry accessible to a wide-ranging audience".

Conversely, scholarship on Queyras is comfortable interpreting her work without being overtaken by personality. Erin Wunker reads the larger form of *Expressway* as taking yet another step forward from the constant flux, or dissolution of boundary between subject and object (such as that Zelazo finds in *Lemon Hound*). Wunker too draws on Deleuze and Guattari, arguing that *Expressway* "jam[s] the traditional lyric transmission"—making subjectivity "an object of discovery" and the poem itself the metaphorical vehicle with which one might find it. In Wunker's formulation, the possibility for change exists within Queyras' challenging of the "dialectical and syntactical strategies of the loved lyric" and her alternative of a more representative "desiring-expressway that teems with endless cars"—in other words, an acknowledgement that our selves and problems are entangled with systems greater than any lone lyric poet's ability to express or resolve them.

I agree with the above critics' description of Queyras' steps towards an innovative, flux-conscious conception of subjectivity, but I'm not quite sure her formal innovations match this ideological and ultimately content-based politics. For example, Queyras' longer lines are frequently redolent of nothing more innovative than found text, sometimes verging on ultra-talk (as seen in her most recent book, *My Ariel* [2017]). "Endless Inter-States" itself is what one might call conservative in formal terms, consisting of six sections, each of which is a page or two of three-line stanzas, the lines of mostly regular length. (The only variation comes when the first, second, and sixth sections end with a brief, standalone line—itself a regular irregularity.) A poem like this, especially, suggests that there's perhaps something more than personal politics to Marjorie Perloff's comparison, in *Unoriginal Genius* (2010), of Queyras' book with Goldsmith's *Traffic*, in which she dismisses Queyras' "so-called 'original' writing" for being "too familiar" and unable to contain the "element of genuine surprise" arising from the unexpected juxtapositions and quotidian oddities found in Goldsmith's lengthy tracts of unoriginality.

Starnino's "San Pellegrino", meanwhile, is meter-conscious, but only in the sense of the pacing and hard-to-quantify "sound impact" of its lines and phrases. What some disparagingly refer to as Starnino's "neoformalism" would perhaps better be described as a poetics defined less by the metre or closed forms of previous American formalisms than by a strict separation of sonic qualities from literal meaning and, via the subtle interplay of these two elements on the level of the individual line, an intuitive intellectual and aesthetic effect. Starnino's many spirited, though ultimately subjective, articulations of this formalism tend to connote strength or efficiency (i.e. his own stated preferences of strength, spontaneity, or musicality)—a slipperiness that, I believe, speaks to his ability to adapt form to the specificities of feeling as opposed to being constrained by it.

Fittingly, "San Pellegrino" splits the difference between formal regularity and a shaping of repeating structural features according to the emotion and narrative pacing of the poem. It consists of nine stanzas of varying length, each of which includes between one and three indented lines. But even these play with the typographical convention, with some indents representing a long line that continues past the margin ("I sit here facing a glass of water doing its level best to conjure [/] his low, unhappy laughter") and others beginning a new sentence following a full stop and therefore functioning more as a separate unit than a continuation of the sense or sound of the original line ("I sit here facing a glass of water. I have a family: a son, baby daughter. / Life's harder. Harder, and sadder. My father"). This subtle yet hard-to-pin-down variation, as well as the visual raggedness that comes from it and the two noticeably longer, thirteen-line stanzas, seems to emphasize the constructedness of the very formal regularity Starnino has long been noted, and criticized, for adhering to.

Still, we're talking about a lyric poem, written in (again) a regularly irregular stanza form; while we may be surprised to find a hint of playfulness in Starnino, or a certain conservatism in Queyras, neither poem is notably adventurous in terms of its form. So I want now to look at where they *do* differ: in their content. "Endless Inter-States" begins with an ominous, unspecific "They" who "go down" "passing / By the glass-pickers, the Geiger counters, those // Guarding the toxic wastes" while remembering "the glide of automobiles, the / Swelter of children in back seats, pinching, twitching, // Sand in their bathing suits, / two-fours of Molson's / In the trunk of the car". Initial capitals aiding the regularity of the poem's stanza form, Queyras' seemingly standard lyric includes a disruptive element on the level of content—the gender-neutral or epicene "they" is immediately surrounded or enveloped by the garbage and radioactive waste of the omnipresent hinterland of the expressway, barred to pedestrians, where family memories are at once placed within the acceptable network of roadways (i.e. the beer "in the trunk") and similarly general. Still on the first page, and within the regular stanza arrangement, these unmarked figures "imagine / Futures they will inhabit, beautiful futures // Filled with unimagined species, new varieties of / Plant life". The first section ends by subdividing the "they" into a speaker addressing a "you". This additional degree of specificity implies companionship, partnership, or desire without adding further identity markers, but it also stays firmly within the boundaries of lyric poetry's at least partially unified speaker-figure.

Section two further blurs identity, specifying a subject's gender but also blending human, non-human animal, and ecology. Beginning, "Web-toed she walks into the land, fins / Carving out river bottoms, each hesitation / A lakebed", the focus here shifts to the third person. The identity and agency of the subject expand to include, respectively, a somewhat specific gender and an ability to construct (or reconstruct) landscape out of an expressway-hinterland that is commonly ignored or forbidden. The third-person pronouns and questioning, implicit "I" of subsequent sections ("Which lifetime? Beyond what brawn? Who / Knew where the road would take us?") contains this variety of perspective, and limited blurring of subject and object, within the traditionally expansive, contingent unity of the lyric subject. The middle of the poem is a catalogue of the roadway's detritus, after which its final section explores the ambiguous possibilities of transgression within the confines of modernity's social norms, concluding, "If it ain't broke / Don't fix, if it ain't resistant, don't / Wince, if it fits like a boot, then boot it. // And so she does". The content here seems to acknowledge that the poem's push to remake a scarred Anthropocene wasteland in conjunction with its recovery of radical individual dignity and particularity pushes against its capacious, but entirely conventional, lyric register. One could even argue that Helen Vendler's description (from *Soul Says*) of the "sonata" of lyric, with its chorus of unified-but-not voices and perspectives all bound by an identifiable "aesthetic signature", is here used to its fullest extent to address multiple and shifting identitarian and ecological perspectives.

"San Pellegrino", on the other hand, like many of its author's poems, is concerned with the nuclear family. The first stanza states, "My father / has Stage IV lung cancer. He's dying, only faster"; the second immediately celebrates the father's idiosyncrasies and flaws: "A fashion sense that hated anything 'fancy schmancy'— anti-dapper. / And such theatre! Talk back, and he'd hike his eyebrows in anger". The failings become more serious, progressing from drunkenness to landing in jail after trying to bribe a traffic cop to failing to pay the rent, sending his wife to "dicker with the landlord" after "put[ting] her through the wringer". By the poem's midpoint, he has "never lost his posture, salvaged a certain swagger / from every blunder. Failure, for my father, was a triumph of style. He was // a beautiful loser". Starnino's signature internal rhymes and quick consonance at once absolve and recreate the father's flawed, theatrical masculinity.

But the second half of the poem exhibits still more self-reflexivity, exploring the speaker's very different set of failings. It begins, "I was the artsy brooder who thought him too dumb for culture. / I always corrected his grammar". In the penultimate stanza, Starnino's meter uncharacteristically bloats out, finally stammering in an acknowledgement that the speaker's facility with words has occluded his ability to appreciate his father's ability to appreciate: "We hugged once and, for a tender second, I thought he'd say something further. / He didn't, afraid perhaps it would seal the matter. ... One way or another, we all fail each other. / But I let that almost-moment be a marker that there was a there, there". This formal doubling makes for a multivalent engagement with the failings of self and other, all couched within, as we would expect, an acceptance of the father's behaviour and the inescapable ugliness of the patriarch. Despite the ostensible conservatism betrayed by Starnino's form, in "San

Pellegrino" a comparative formal complexity or innovation is the vessel that carries, and emphasizes, an ideological traditionalism (which could be, and has been, uncharitably regarded as white heteronormativity).

It seems, then, that Queyras uses a more regular free-verse form to depict a transcendence or reshaping of gender, family, genealogy and ecology, while Starnino is in fact slightly more formally adventurous, using the arbitrariness of line and typography to express his more conservative content. To play off the within-and-against construction, Queyras stays *within* traditional free-verse and a regular stanza sequence to work *against* social convention, whereas Starnino pushes *against* the rote formalism precisely to emphasize that his questioning of social convention remains largely *within* those conventions. Whether you agree or disagree with my chiasmus, the larger point here is that we can map the work of these supposed polar opposites within the same, fairly restricted field of (at least formal) understanding. "Endless Inter-States" and "San Pellegrino" would, from this perspective, appear to be cut from very similar cloth; it's hard to see how they occupy alternate poetic or ethical universes—or, how either could be considered particularly radical (or, for that matter, blandly conventional).

I'm aware that this argument is somewhat myopic; it falls apart to some extent when one considers that each of the above poems is a distinct work within a book-length sequence, and that much of the other poetry in *Expressway* looks a good deal more different from that surrounding "San Pellegrino" as it appears in *Leviathan*. I think it's notable, however, that Wunker's article reads closely just about every section of the book except for "Endless Inter-States". So while individual poems like the two I've discussed are perhaps undermining experimental-traditional distinctions, the larger works in which such poems appear continue to reify these distinctions by surrounding such works with either noticeably more fragmented or abstract pieces (in *Expressway*) or else, in Starnino's case, a focus on the discrete, well-crafted poem. But, as I've outlined above regarding critical engagements with Starnino's work, we're now in the realm of generalizations—

casual observations about large bodies of work, swaths of criticism, personalities, attitudes, and the self-presentation that inheres in any publishing enterprise as well as even the most minor poet or critic's social positioning, in real life or online. I want to suggest only that at least some of these givens may begin to erode if we get into the nuts and bolts of specific poems themselves.

That said, I'm also being intentionally provocative. I'm well aware that arguing for similarity—for a lack of nuance, or singularity, or incomparability—is perhaps anathema to the practice of literary criticism. But I thought I'd give it a try to see what doors it opens up, especially given the apples-and-oranges nature of any comparison of the larger personas and poetics of the authors in question. If I've achieved anything with this reading, perhaps it's to ask what we actually mean when we rely on generalizations that are safe or accepted, as opposed to provocative or born of a devil's-advocate impulse—that is, when we describe a poet as experimental, or innovative, or traditional, or conservative. I've begun to suspect, and perhaps my brief comparison illustrates, that these words are inflected by another elastic, although more politically valent, term—"progressive"—more than any durable, enduring, easy-to-distinguish connection with formal characteristics.

State of the Avant:
Checking in on Experimental Literature

Thomas Hodd's *#NoMoreNotes*, the previously discussed manifesto against the proliferation of notes at the end of poetry collections, wonders why a range of contemporary poets make such notation when lyric poets of the past felt no need. When anticipating the objection that such notes add information that helps readers understand more of the poems in question, Hodd considers other art forms: "But hold on: painters don't include such information with their paintings, or sculptors, or playwrights, or the vast majority of short story writers... I could go on, but you get the picture". I appreciate his take on the rapidly increasing number of notes sections, but this particular position gives the impression that Hodd may not have been to a contemporary art gallery in a while, for the bloviating nightmare that is the contemporary visual artist's statement comes across as far more of an offence against the impact of the work itself than any notes section I've paged through with (admittedly) waning interest.

It's a strange omission, given that Hodd lists a few possible reasons for the poetry-note explosion. One reason, however, sheds light not on the state of contemporary poetry or painting as much as a larger mode, or class, or niche, that has joined and increasingly defined areas of both worlds. Back to Hodd:

> The fourth, and perhaps most disturbing reason is that the scholarization of poets through the granting of creative-

writing degrees has [led] them to feel compelled to make their projects more credible in the eyes of academics, and so they are encouraged, perhaps intentionally or subconsciously, to include a Notes section because it will add more scholarly weight when it comes time for thesis defence. Of course, in such a scenario the Notes section becomes nothing more than an academic smokescreen to help legitimize Creative Writing programs to university administrations. And with this reason, we have a death knell to poetry itself: poets are writing for incorporation into the academy than for the pursuit of art.

I would go even further in this direction and identify as the problem not any MFA industry but a larger institutionalization of culture—that is, a more pervasive tendency to locate a work of art within some kind of progressively oriented, unified aesthetic theory. This larger zeitgeist validates Hodd's earlier suspicion that wanting to treat the experiences and reading behind a poem as research is the result of "having written too many grant proposals for an increasingly business-minded cultural industry". While there are, of course, camps of scholars vs. creative writers, a larger system now structures poems themselves, not only shielding them from a larger public but reshaping the art itself so that it's only recognizable to a few select breeds of quasi-expert. If, as I have been suggesting in these pages, the weirdness of a poem is its simultaneous recognizability and ineffability, even unclassifiability, then the problem is that all of this is already happening with any poem. Why insist on codifying a subset of contemporary poems as more logical, or academic, or in keeping with experimental lineages? Perhaps it's done just for the sake of grants or tenure, as Hodd points out when it comes to notes. Or, to take Hodd's criticism further, their listing these things as procedure is meant to accrue experimental cred—not unlike when a rock-radio band on the wave of mainstreaming a trend that used to be called indie cites as influences commonly namedropped predecessors whose music sounded nothing like theirs.

This isn't so different from how standard conceptions of the canon work: we want to be both pathbreakers and experts, so we take people like Joyce—just weird enough to be cool in the context of an undergraduate course on modernism—and talk about them as though they're exemplary. Any notion of a canon, perhaps aside from identity-based counter-canons (which are contradictory insofar as those proposing them often purport to reject the concept of a canon in whatever larger sense it hegemonically or previously existed), skews this way, emphasizing traces of the weird or the prescient even as it presents its materials as a set of norms. These notions of the canon can overlap somewhat neatly with periods of time (Romantic poetry, Victorian novels), or they can coexist with other, more widely accepted modes of the age, like capital-*m* Modernism. Looking back at the 1920s, what writer wouldn't today want to have been one of the High Modernist elect?

But there's a problem when that desire extends into the present and, especially, beyond whatever writing one's actually doing. Michael Robbins' "Ripostes" (2013) took issue with this, mocking a nebulous and yet, already at the time of his writing, somewhat maligned formation called "the postmodern"—not so much Canada's vaguely politicized, vaguely descriptive variants,[1] but rather a more diverse swath of writing that, in its American and Language-based variants, somehow came to be regarded as alternative or other even as those modes became dominant forms of poetic expression. This is the dynamic Robbins attacks when he impugns the 2013 expanded second edition of Paul Hoover's *Postmodern American Poetry: A Norton Anthology*, chiding, "You will note the absence of a *Norton Anthology of Mainstream Poetry*" and referring to the dreaded m-word as "a construction of today's soi-disant 'avant-garde,' which is a construction of poets in love with their image of themselves as perennial outsiders".[2]

---

1   I take as the most prominent of these Linda Hutcheon's historiographic metafiction, which she defines in *The Canadian Postmodern* as writing in which the "self-consciousness of art *as art* is paradoxically made the means to a new engagement with the social and historical world, and that this is done in such a way as to challenge (though not destroy) our traditional humanist beliefs about the function of art in society". I use the term *vague* in the main text because of what today reads like a contradiction between the defined and prescribed mode of literary-historical engagement and the supposedly radical search for alternate histories that characterizes Canadian instances of historiographic metafiction.

2   Rereading it seven years out, Robbins' attack is at once refreshing and indicative of the extent to which mainstream-experimental divisions have further

The scare quotes Robbins puts around "avant-garde" indicate that he's talking about a larger and fuzzier entity, much like whatever contemporary writing one might be referring to today as *postmodernist*. But the situation of what's more clearly demarcated, at least in Canada, as a contemporary avant-garde (now that we're here, let's go with *AG*) has more than a little in common with the contradiction Robbins apprehends better than Hoover does. Yes, the AG means something other than *somewhat newer* or *somewhat more interesting to younger cohorts of poetry students*. It is a defined set of poetic practices. The problem, for me, is that insisting on the meaning of the term seems to derive from a degree of self-obsession. It's a set of practices that has been almost fully absorbed into poetry the hardest of the hard avant-garde would describe as irrelevant lyric. I can't remember the last time I picked up a recent book of poetry that didn't include found or repurposed text and—to return to Hodd—wasn't at pains to let me know this was the case in the form of an explanatory note. The actual poems inside any number of these books don't bear out the notion that there's a core of writers meaningfully innovative or even different enough to mark everyone else as trapped in bygone poetic traditions. But many seem invested in maintaining precisely this picture.

A Sample of Self-Justification

Take, for example, the very existence of a book called *Experimental Literature: A Collection of Statements* (2018). The book's premise—the statements are in defense of the avant-garde, made by practitioners and preachers of the avant—shows us this insistence on upholding the distinction. Editors Jeffrey R. Di Leo and Warren Motte, in going with the term "statements", leave at least some degree of ambiguity regarding the common purpose of the essays they've collected. And indeed, they state near the beginning of their introduction that the designation "sometimes gets a bad rap", and that many working in the mode

---

collapsed. It's harder today to imagine a poet as ensconced in the academy and on leftist Twitter the way Robbins is make comments like "Hoover has bought into [Flarf] wholesale, along with Kenneth Goldsmith's so-called conceptualism, Brian Kim Stefans' 'cyberpoetry,' and the whole boatload of vacuous bullshit".

(although none of those who contribute to the book) accept the label only reluctantly. Then again, the formulation does exactly what Robbins' falsely embattled postmodernists do: it shows us that capital-e Experimental writing, and most especially writing that calls itself avant-garde, is under attack on all sides. From conservatives, philistines, the neoliberal academy, non-experimental minority literatures that are themselves under threat—even self-loathing experimentalists themselves.

One wonders, as Robbins does, what the institution of experimental writing would look like if stripped of its claims of marginalization. Would it exist in the form of perceptibly different stylistic elements? Different politics? If so, can a book like *Experimental Literature* show us any substance in the notoriously slippery category on which it insists? Given the intensifying cultural myopia in pretty much everyone's bubble, somebody approaching the topic from critical distance could be forgiven for wondering if such a collection would be able to engage in good faith with this state of affairs.

The book, an expanded version of a 2016 issue of *American Book Review*, acknowledges the contradiction at times, but its answer comes in the form of another contradiction: namely, that it manages somehow to provide nearly three hundred pages of insights in formally varied prose without successfully demonstrating the distinctness of the entity the essays are supposed to validate and comprise. The statements are incredibly intelligent, often hard-hitting, and at times thought provoking. But, at least if one reads the book with that central problem in mind, it's also *maddening*, adding new dimensions to the central paradoxes at the heart of experimental writing but proving unable to break free from them.

To its credit, the book includes some disarmingly frank discussions. Kenneth Goldsmith's "Poetry is Not Public Policy" reads like a response to the fall from conceptualist grace that followed his 2015 reading of "The Body of Michael Brown". After running through now familiarly paradoxical statements about poetry's powerlessness (its "power is its powerlessness, which is the power to imagine the unimaginable", etc.), Goldsmith gets more explicit, stating,

pataphysics is a bad way to conduct social justice. In the real
world, real solutions are required for real problems. This is not
poetry's work. Poetry's work is to jam systems with irrationality,
with illogic and abstraction.

Even if shifting the conversation to culture-jamming feels
like another attempt at rebranding oneself an outsider among
outsiders, direct, honest statements about what poetry (and words
generally) can and cannot do are much needed among progressive
arts communities. This is an instance of the AG doing what so
many others won't or can't. But the sentiment, and Goldsmith
himself, are sufficiently controversial to call into question the
extent to which it's representative of anything we might call
collectively experimentalist. Steve Tomasula's "I Joined the Avant-
Garde to Save the World and All I Got Was This Goofy Red Hat"
does something similar, engaging directly with what many of us
know but would be hesitant to tweet about—that the Orwellian, "it
means whatever I want it to mean" language tricks of the Trump
administration are a direct descendent of the postmodernist ideas
that have been circulated for decades by well-meaning progressives
teaching at colleges and universities. Yet few (at least in Canada)
would make the argument that such unwantedly trenchant social
critique describes much of what we call the AG.

There's also the familiar myopia. Even just on a stylistic
or rhetorical level, "this is experimental lit" touchstones are
maddeningly consistent. Early on, a self-interview by Mark
Amerika follows a format that's cloying and self-important no
matter how ostensibly ironized; Charles Bernstein's piece, which
initially reads like an interview, plays the same predictable self-as-
other game (even if it concludes with characteristically penetrating
insights on poetry's dual ability to foster critical thought and
remain distinct from the practical). Goldsmith's statement is far
from the only one that doubles and triples down on paradox and
chiasmus: lines like "Literature as that which has standardized its
refusal of standardization" at this point seem attributable to some
phantom avant-garde brain trust as opposed to any author.

And then there's the alphabet. With the exception of an
introduction by the editors and Robert Coover's afterword, the
book is organized alphabetically, by contributor's surname.

Perhaps it's strange to criticize such a minor organizational point, especially one that makes finding specific essays more convenient while also ensuring contributors aren't ordered according to prestige. It's just that I've read dozens, seemingly hundreds, of so-called experimental works that take the alphabet as their primary inspiration, or means of organization, or subject matter, or whatever. I understand the appeal of the system for those with AG interests—the alphabet is at once arbitrary and systematic, rudimentary and genealogically complex, ostensibly neutral and yet deeply coded on cultural levels. But it's also all of these things every single time *another* concrete poem, or sequence of poems, or entire book fixates on it. Can repeated engagement with something so omnipresent as the alphabet really be considered a hallmark of innovation?

Hold on—we're back at paradox with that last term. So here's another one: it seems to me that some swaths of the avant-garde are at this point unquestioningly reverent of experimentalist touchstones. Considering this type of oxymoronic experimental traditionalism (or the traditionally experimental, to be chiasmatic), it could, however tastelessly, be described as the most conservative contemporary literary category I've encountered. To return to *Experimental Literature*, Alan Singer's "Norms and Experimental Knowing" acknowledges this contradiction by productively examining the relationship between norms and the unexpected. Singer suggests that "norms do not inexorably make a dogma of knowledge" but are rather "its condition of possibility". He adds a reader-response element to his take, arguing compellingly that the "signature shock" of the avant-garde "is little more than recognition that one's fragile expectations have been revealed in all of their fragility". By the end of the essay, however, he too lapses into sloganeering that seems generated solely for the sake of vaguely chiasmatic sonic resonance, concluding an out-of-nowhere extolment of Henry Green with a line about being Green's being "an epitome of how normative predictability is inextricable from knowing the unpredictable".

There are statements in the book that reach well beyond the coterie, but the length they go introduces another problem with defining the AG. Christina Milletti's take on distant reading and technologically oriented literature strengthens the collection's real-world engagement. Its discussion of the way military research uses narrative—notably, guessable plot points—to predict real events yields a deeply unsettling version of the affirmation that literature really does matter; or, that "If, conventionally, fiction has exploited the realm of fact for its purposes, it's not too much to say that, now, the realm of fact has begun to exploit fiction". The statements that seem most compelling are the ones that harness the rich heritage of experimental writing for the purpose of engaging with something other than itself.

But many others that reach this far make only large, arbitrary claims that don't hold much water. Singer begins with the everything-and-nothing aphorism, "Is literature ever *not* experimental?" Ostensibly more specific yet still more arbitrary and hyperbolic is Carole Maso's claim that silence is "something formulaic writing blithely ignores". Broadly "literary" writing can certainly be understood as distinct from, say, genre fiction or blockbuster movies. But it's difficult to conceive of these formats—turning as so many do on commonplace yet nevertheless complex mechanisms like dialogue—as somehow not being attuned to silence. (That Maso refers to the latter as "that thing at the heart of all expression" makes the claim especially puzzling.) An even bigger stretch is Steve McCaffery's "positing of an alliance between feminism, romanticism and experimental literature"—a move that's experimental in that it could have resulted from picking two keywords out of a hat. Which could itself be making a point, but probably not the one the editors were going for (at least based on the earnestness of their introduction to the project).

There's another strange irony in these attempts to be expansive without abandoning the AG's singularity. Several of the book's arguments get too close to basic essay-writing "don'ts" taught to students in English departments. Brian Evenson's "Notes on Experimental Writing" considers which of two anthologies better represents experimentalism, concluding that "the experimental nature of a piece is highly dependent on the particularities of a given reader"—a thoughtful take, but one that's strikingly similar to the claim frequently made in first-year essays that "it's up to the reader to decide". Motte's own essay makes the convincing claim that experimental writing should be designated as such if it forces us to alter our reading practices. But even this take, when combined with statements like "When we read, we are neither subject nor object exclusively", veers a little too close to the vague, sophomoric claim that x piece of writing "draws the reader in".

"Viewpoint diversity" has become a taboo phrase among progressives, who increasingly interpret it as calling for the inclusion of far-right viewpoints in intellectual discourse (and, by somewhat logical extension, the concomitant legitimation of such ideas). But I don't think it's at all insidious, or out of step with progressive notions of diversity[3] to point out a similar lack of diversity here: namely, that, by my count, twenty-six of the thirty-six contributor bios make explicit reference in their essays to their affiliations with post-secondary institutions. Several of those that don't mention an affiliation list at least one work published by a university press. Many of the essays draw at length on these experiences with university teaching and administration. These facts make it especially ironic that the collection returns so frequently to what professors, instructors, and Teaching Assistants tell their students are irrelevant approaches or irresolvable questions. More troublingly, the numbers articulate quite well in themselves where experimental literature exists, or at least where it's confirmed as relevant.

That the entire phantom category of the AG exists in such close proximity to the academy makes another emergent conflict seem inevitable—that is, the differences between, on the one hand, a formally defined and preoccupied area of writing, and, on the other, the emphasis on identity and social justice that pervades so much of the arts and humanities. In addition to Goldsmith's piece, Bök's contribution, the multi-sectioned "Statements", begins by doubling down on paradox and chiasmus, yet with a degree of directness, even anger, as well as a knowing wink ("About Plagiarists" includes lines like "Those who cannot learn from poetry are condemned to repeat it"). "About Readerships" attacks

---

3   I will note here that just over half of the volume's contributors appear to be white, cisgender men.

what Bök calls conceptualism's "'unthinkership' of reactionaries", who "prefer the security of 'groupthink' rather than the fortuity of iconoclasm"; by the time he gets to "About Hatemongers", his sights are unmistakably set on the more aggressive iterations of online progressivism. Statements like "Writers who cannot lay claim to their talent always lay claim to their virtue" and "The autocratic, the censorious, are never social, always unjust" ridicule group-oriented and political approaches to literature. It's inflammatory, and its force is palpable. Yet even this most hostile of Bök's salvos chooses to tie its disapprobation into the type of knot we'd expect from a classical avant-gardist: "The mob metaphorically 'lynches' the poet for using the word 'lynches' metaphorically".

The book's final two essays—Anne Waldman's "Epic Experiment: Praetexa & Performance" and Robert Coover's afterword, "The End of Literature"—treat this emergent conflict in different ways, or at least using different terms. Waldman shifts from poetry to an exploration of past experimentalists' formal techniques of being "contemporary with their time", drawing from Pound, Gertrude Stein, and Paul Celan before locating her own work in this genealogy. By its end, however, the essay is a bit evasive, forging this link not only with reference to the Union Carbide disaster in Bhopal but also with questions about the extent to which experimentalism is now synonymous with identity and the incomparability of personal experience. Coover asks early on whether "literature itself is an expiring holdover from the last century, using an outmoded technology and fast declining into an archival state of primary interest only to scholars and hobbyists, the current worldwide proliferation of writing programs nothing but a death rattle?" Ultimately, however, he states that basically everyone and everything is post-literature, which will continue to carry out "all the grand endeavors we associate with literature, even if what they make may not be literature, any more than film is literature or nature a poem".

Which would be a much-needed perspective, even if considering only the technological issues he outlines. But, however literary or post-literary it is, does this greater era of harmony and fluidity—of identity but also in terms of the breaking down of boundaries between forms, disciplines, arts, in some cases even art and science—leave any room for what we call literature? Or for what we call experimental?

Things today seem still more confused. The cultural leveling Coover refers to—engendered, I think, by the pedagogical innovations and cultural-studies approaches of literary-academic communities, not to mention the pressure to collapse our omnivorous cultural consumption and multimodal approaches into identifiable online versions of ourselves—makes it seem as if traces of the experimental are pretty much everywhere. I've read poetry books that are stamped as Officially Avant-Garde and whose style and compositional techniques are borrowed directly from the 1980s. Recent books by Adam Dickinson (2006's *Kingdom, Phylum*, especially) and Ken Hunt (*The Manhattan Project*, 2020) seem to consist of lyric poetry that draws from lists of technical terms—these too get the stamp. I've also come across books by supposedly rigid, formally conservative reactionaries that are far more inventive than those of younger poets whose experimentalism seems to consist of mentioning the Internet a lot (see the previous two essays).

Yet there remain those who insist on the label—those who staunchly self-identify as AG, seeking to highlight their uniqueness and their relevance. Accordingly, it's also not too difficult to imagine that there are writers out there—beginners, failures, whatever—who wish nothing more than to be known as experimental or avant-garde, whose writing may even resonate with whatever broadly accepted formal characteristics survive close, intelligent scrutiny (such as that collected in *Experimental Literature*) but who are not accepted into the fold. However arbitrary the construction, as is the case with many things, one important criterion—the most important?—is that an experimental writer be validated as such by other experimental writers. If I'm correct in identifying some tension between experimental and identity-centric literary camps, this is certainly a new paradox to add to the list.

Taking any kind of broad view of the literature being written right now, there are of course clusters of authors with broadly different sets of influences and values. And, admittedly, it's hard to imagine disciples of Bök or Goldsmith being scandalized by a serial paraphraser, like when, in late 2018, parts of the US poetry world erupted upon revelations that someone named Ailey O'Toole had too closely mimicked the structure and content of several recent poems by her peers.[4] That said, once one starts looking at actual poems at the centre of the muddled, maybe-pomo literary universe Robbins describes, it just isn't accurate to state that there's a cluster of poets whose practice is either so meaningfully different or meaningfully unified as to warrant a title that marks everyone not in this group as irrelevant or mired in tradition. Di Leo and Motte's introduction itself pulls back from this claim, suggesting instead that "experimental writing is like any cultural phenomenon in our time—only more so". The problem is that the claim they make instead is so capacious and arbitrary that it makes one wonder whether it's productive to gather such wildly varied work into any singular category. It's yet another instance in which the insistence on the importance of the category is the problem.

We can identify a historical avant-garde, surely. And, while some writers will continue to draw inspiration from it for some time to come, we ought to acknowledge that things change. We can—so many younger writers I encounter already do—draw from some precedents and discard others, just as they alternately incorporate or ignore the identities and experiences we're dealt. Doing so shouldn't come with the feeling that we're either betraying or securing membership in some sclerotic coterie or outlook—especially when that group defines itself precisely in being indefinable as a group. Unless, that is, we're willing to redefine group identity less as static and politicized in the conventional sense and more as shifting and involving the situational allegiances with which the networking individual chooses (or chooses not) to identify.

---

4   See Flood, "Prize-nominated poet's debut cancelled as plagiarism accusations build", which outlines accusations by Rachel McKibbens that led to the cancellation of O'Toole's debut collection. The controversy seems all the more preposterous when viewed from the angle of conceptual writing given the identity-centric nature of McKibbens' complaint as well as the fact that O'Toole, in what was either a display of extreme self-delusion or a masterful embodiment of the spirit of uncreative writing and its impulse to reformat, had the offending lines tattooed on her arm.

Avant and the Future

Gregory Betts and Christian Bök, in their introduction to *Avant Canada: Poets, Prophets, Revolutionaries* (2019), state that untimeliness is what defines the Canadian avant-garde. Always too early or too late, the avant-garde in this country especially confronts the temporal contradictions and interruptions inherent in the term itself ("avant" signifying both *before* and *beyond*) in the form of its "waves of vanguards". Then there's a jarring move: after observing that Canada as a nation-state has existed for as long as the avant-garde as we know it, they point out that the first appearance of the term *avant garde* in a Canadian context comes from the memoirs of Louis-Armand, Baron de Lahontan, who in 1703 used it to refer to elite groups of Haudenosaunee fighters.

It's jarring because the act of making the case for a Canadian avant that is still meaningfully avant requires a sleight of hand: a French memoir from over a century before any meaningful avant-garde existed, as well as the Indigenous armies it refers to, partake of the tradition; "magpie" contemporary authors drawing from multiple traditions (experimental and less so), meanwhile, are almost dismissed as part of Reginald Shepherd's conception of the "post-avant".[1] It's the same contradiction outlined in the previous essay, and it emerges again when Betts and Bök define four types of the avant: concrete poetics, Language Writing, identity writing, and copyleft poetics. It's a convincing

---

1   Betts and Bök refer to Shepherd's "Who You Callin' 'Post-Avant'?"

taxonomy of some Canadian writing that has emerged in the last five decades, but how the Canadian case exists as a separate avant realm is unclear. For example, concrete poetry appears to some degree in all kinds of contemporary poetry collections; Language Writing is now mainstream poetry; identity writing, is if anything, the dominant mode in today's Canadian poetry, and much of it is formally conservative.

The sometimes-remarked social determinants of experimental poetry, despite being or at least seeming exclusionary, also open some new possibilities for creating positive change within the worsening conditions of life under neoliberalism. Let's consider a recent shift in which avant-garde poetry is seen less as inherently political and more as inherently collaborative (that's from Stephen Voyce, *Poetic Community*), or even, as Felix Bernstein writes in *Notes on Post-Conceptual Poetry*, defined by social vicissitudes to such an extent that participation in these poetry scenes reorganizes the "boundaries that separate work from play, art from life". As cynical as these matters might seem, I think this expanded field of networks and the choices poets and commentators make still have a kind of potential. That is to say, the arbitrary, social shifts that seem to determine how poets conceive of and present their own work as well as what they choose to engage with critically, and how, could be a case for the ongoing distinctness of something that still ought to be called the avant-garde. What's more, the situational, social element that's at play in conceptions and practices of the avant does the opposite of what I've argued the markedly accessible work of Rupi Kaur does. The avant-garde's emphasis on the arbitrary and its half-systematization in the clique, in other words, means that its supposed potential for radicalism is socially conservative in the same way that Kaur's homespun simplicity is radically inclusive due to its accessibility.

While Voyce and Bernstein are ambivalent about this latter phenomenon, Brian Fawcett made some similar, albeit far more pessimistic, statements against Vancouver experimentalists and the politics of Language Poetry more generally in his 1991 essay, "East Van Uber Alles?" Fawcett compares two types of "oppositional" writing—one political (Tom Wayman and the Vancouver Industrial Writers Union) and one formal (Language

Writing, or, as he abbreviates it, LCW). His case against the latter
(generally, with the Kootenay School of Writing as a Canadian/
BC exponent) is as follows: "They [that is, Charles Bernstein, Ron
Silliman, and Bruce Andrews] seem to know what LCW isn't,
but are unable or unwilling to state clearly what it does do that
other poetic methods haven't. Maybe they're afraid that some
brontosaurus is going to stand up and say, 'Well, isn't this just a
super-complicated attempt to make poetry a public act without
demanding that it also be socially interactive communication?'".
He offers an "[u]nkindly translated" version of an attempt at a
definition from Andrews:

> LCW is a device based on a rhetorical unification of the communicator
> and the target of communication so as to give both the outward
> appearance of egalitarian community and intellectual coherence
> without any of the responsibilities of either community or coherence.

Fawcett ultimately concludes that Canadian iterations of
Language Writing are thus premised on exclusion. In closing,
he anticipates Godwin's law years before widespread Internet
connectivity, thus resigning himself to angry-man obsolescence
decades in advance: such "Kabbalas and secret societies", he
says, are attempts "to exclude—and when their members start
wearing uniforms and carrying guns, to exterminate—whatever
they can't control".

In describing the avant-gardist's cynical or malevolent
desire to exclude, however, Fawcett may have uncovered at
least the possibility of a way out of neoliberalism's containment
of novelty. Fawcett's piece anticipates by twenty-five years
Bernstein's commentary on the ideology behind the overlapping
poetry and visual arts scenes in contemporary New York City.
Bernstein's distinction (mentioned previously) between first-
generation conceptualism and post-conceptual poetry involves
regarding the latter as bringing "affect, emotion, and ego" back
into the "empty networking structures" that define the former.
The result of such a jaded reassertion of affect, emotion, and ego,
is at its core self-serving. As Bernstein scathingly puts it,

> the post-conceptual poet must keep attempting to add exhaustion
> to the content of the work. If one actually abandons the machinery

of Facebook and Twitter and networking and queeronormative identities one is cut out of the archive altogether. That is to say, only happy dandies (they can be exhausted, queer, or crippled as long as they are 'happy') can and do succeed in this economy.

Paradoxically (or not), an argument like Fawcett's is coming from Bernstein fils (date of birth 1992), who, as son of Charles, is more "on the inside" than anyone else.

According to Felix Bernstein, then, we all have to play the happy game or else risk being taken off the invite list. This sounds terrible, but is it a different kind of terrible than the neoliberal realities of the avant-garde I alluded to before? As stated earlier, in relation to the expansive nature of Rupi Kaur's writing, Paul Mann has emphasized the avant-garde's recuperation of margins and the result—that the "death of the avant-garde is its theory and the theory of the avant-garde is its death". Despite my earlier complaints about the chiasmus as copout, Mann's formulation expresses the totality of the recuperative economy as well as its concomitant containment of any possibility of radicalism, negativity, or incongruity.

Mann is unpopular, at least insofar as I don't see him cited that much. Which probably means that his insights a) are somewhat uncomfortable, and b) may be correct in some visceral sense. So, if we who produce or appreciate work that is seen as avant-garde are indeed becalmed amid the death of theory and the theorization of our death, in which anything is eligible for recuperation and discussion, then suddenly the ability to exclude on social grounds—that is to say, arbitrarily—becomes a method of disruption. It's hard to disagree that pretty much anything can be recuperated, but only after a long time. Recuperation in the future depends entirely on exclusion in the present. What's more, Mann himself alludes to this potential for resistance by acknowledging that celebration, commemoration, and then recuperation are carried out by a network of socially-located scholars and supporters. Even as the system seems increasingly total, not just anyone can do the approving or rehabilitating.

Which brings me to Christian Bök, whose criticism simultaneously validates Canada's traces of an early avant-garde and constructs this category as a means of excluding so-called "mainstream" Canadian writers. In his afterword to *Ground Works: Avant-Garde for Thee* (2002), Bök finds examples of Canadian avant-garde fiction, but states explicitly that such authors

> do not constitute a coherent movement of consistently experimental writers whose entire oeuvre brims with innovative iconoclasm. On the contrary, these works constitute a brief encyclopedia of millenary potential, whose possibilities still await further exploration and further development by a subsequent generation of storytellers.

Bök relies on critical exposition to tease out the experimentalism he's assembled in the collection.

It's no surprise, then, that Bök the poet takes this commitment to "further exploration and further development" a step further, perhaps with more of a twist than is evident in his broad, generative call to "storytellers". The conceit of his *Xenotext* (2015) is Bök's producing a pair of poems, "Orpheus" and "Eurydice", that "encode" each other; each letter of the alphabet is substituted by another letter. Then, each letter in the poems is assigned a DNA codon to make a chemically viable gene, which is inserted into a microbe, in which the inserted gene creates a new protein, whose chemical structure can be decoded as the second poem. This is hard enough to explain, right? Now imagine how many pages it might fill rendered as academic writing. Brent Raycroft (whose description I basically paraphrased here), in a review of *The Xenotext Vol. 1*, goes through possible objections to the project:

> Cryptographers might point out that Bök could not have examined a fraction of the mono-alphabetic ciphers available to him (there are roughly 8 trillion) and must have chosen certain word pairs himself for convenience and aesthetics. Geneticists might argue that if a mutation does not give the organism a survival advantage (just a "poem") it would be removed by natural processes and could not outlast a printed book much less the human species... .

Raycroft says he's willing to cut Bök some slack on all these counts, but "[w]hat [he] can't overlook" is Bök's leaving "'Orpheus' and 'Eurydice' out of *The Xenotext Book 1*". The poems themselves have been held back to a second volume. So we have a project—a grant application (or many), descriptions, press, and now a separate volume of poems, all as paratext, promotional materials, etc., in support of the "final event". It's two "future-published" poems preceded by years' worth of paratext.

If we delve into North American poetry more broadly here, we see that Bök's use of description to maximize a project's immediacy (Mann's term) is neither an isolated incident nor some uniquely craven commitment to self-promotion. *Against Expression*, the pioneering 2011 anthology of conceptual writing edited by Kenneth Goldsmith and Craig Dworkin, which includes Canadian writers such as Bök, Derek Beaulieu, Gregory Betts, Bill Kennedy, Darren Wershler, and M. NourbeSe Philip, consists of an introductory section for each author, followed by selections of that author's work. The introductory sections deal with biography, but also, most importantly, the method and concept behind each piece as well as some forays into hermeneutics. Given the highly abstract or seemingly minimalist nature of many of the excerpts themselves—Yedda Morrison's *Kyoto Protocol* consists of its titular document converted into wingdings, for instance, while each of Shigeru Matsui's "Pure Poems" consists of a sequence of the roman numerals for one, two, and three—the interested scholar or generalist could be forgiven for devoting their full attention to the introductory sections of interest, only to skim cursorily through the subsequent, sometimes sparsely populated pages of text.

This arrangement has become the norm in collections of conceptual or otherwise experimental writing, as well as individual collections of experimental poetry. Savvy readers will most likely know to flip to the end first in order to get a better idea of the method behind the madness one will confront if starting to read from page one. (This itself isn't new; I was caught off guard by *not* doing this when I read Dave Godfrey's *I Ching Kanada* [1976].) Members of experimental coteries such as Derek Beaulieu have gotten a lot of mileage out of this kind of descriptive poetics. Appended to the concrete poems of Beaulieu's *Fractal Economies* (2006), for instance, is a scholarly essay/manifesto, "An Afterward after Words: Notes Toward a Concrete Poetic". The prose experiments of Beaulieu's *How to Write* (2010), meanwhile, are explained in a set of notes at the end: "Nothing Odd Can Last" consists of thirty-six alphabetized questions from Coles Notes-style websites on Laurence Sterne's *The Life and Opinions of Tristram Shandy, Gentleman.*[2] The point is that a large part of the resonance of writing such as Bök's depends on its mention by scholars of the avant-garde. Marjorie Perloff, for instance, generates in monograph after monograph a unique history of twentieth century avant-garde artworks that just so happens to culminate in the present-day enterprises of her and Bök's longtime associate, Kenneth Goldsmith.

Bök's critical work *'Pataphysics* is an indirect indication of precisely this dynamic. The book sets out to trace the enduring exceptionality of its subject:

> Each movement revises a prior schema about the structure of exception in order to disrupt the normalization of the 'pataphysical. for the Futurists, exception results from the collision of machines; for the Oulipians, exception results from the constraint of programs; and, for the Jarryites, exception results from the corruption of memories. Like these movements, this survey also tries to avoid the normalization of the 'pataphysical, doing so by alluding intermittently to 'pataphysical enterprises that do not refer to the tradition of Jarry but nevertheless represent some of the exceptions to the genealogy that this survey posits.

The passages that are set up as the book's key points are an unrelenting torrent of paradox and chiasmus. An example: "For 'pataphysics, any science sufficiently retarded in progress must seem magical (but only after the fact), just as any science sufficiently advanced in progress must seem magical (but only before the fact)". Here's my favourite: "Whereas a thematic pedagogue (such as Atwood or Frye) interprets sovereign geography as a metaphysical cipher for a mythic memory (believing such a 'myth' to be true), a rational geomancer interprets memory itself as a 'pataphysical cipher for an imaginary landscape (believing the 'true' to be a myth)". Not since Robert Kroetsch, who is at one point denigrated in the book—nay, perhaps not since Foucault—

---

2   Beaulieu's collection of criticism, *Seen of the Crime* (Snare, 2011), consists largely of this kind of description of other works and poetics; it includes very few passages that could be described as hermeneutical, argumentative, or, I would say, even just "critical" used in its proper definition. A rare exception is his gentle dismissal of bill bissett, which doesn't fit the ideology of description I'm describing. Maybe there's more to that story.

has chiasmus so completely taken the place of conclusion. The book's contribution, or at least effect, is much more aesthetic and celebratory than it is intellectual.

Mann himself acknowledges that Jarry's notion of 'Pataphysics itself demonstrates this dead or totalizing situation: "'Pataphysics not only observes the operation of the laws of exceptionality; it also legislates and enforces them. It is a radical epistemology that produces by witnessing and governs by description, that both describes exception and conscripts the exceptions it describes". "To write or rewrite a theory of the avant-garde", then,

> is thus precisely to engage in 'pataphysics: the 'pataphysician is the proper figure of the theorist-critic of the avant-garde. The theory of the avant-garde is itself a means not only of analyzing or even promoting but of governing a certain border, a certain limit or margin, a certain mode of cultural alterity.

It seems self-defeating, but that disappointment carries within itself the ideal that, depending on your perspective, might make it all worthwhile in some sense. Going back through Jarry and still further, one finds a device that captures this systematization of paradoxes and why it might continue to sustain conceptions of an avant-garde as always ahead or beyond. The clinamen, first conceived by Epicurus and Lucretius as the tendency of atoms to swerve unpredictably, has more recently been understood as the principle of the aleatory or the exception—that is, as the factor that by definition disrupts systems and itself resists systemization. It has come to be held as an ideal by avant-gardists who admire its disruptive possibility. Bök himself unpacks the clinamen as going beyond even any system that "values the norm of difference" in its finding "a way to detour around things in a system that values the fate of contrivance", even as he works throughout 'Pataphysics to systematize the possibility of disrupting systematization.

Considered in these terms, what remains of the clinamen's disruptive possibility? Bök's 'Pataphysics, tongue-in-cheek as it might read, looks more and more like its value lies in (again following Mann's terms) its selective recuperation and reiteration of a chosen set of predecessors—an act that Bök inscribes formally in his reliance on chiasmus. To simplify its function further, the book is a gesture, or an exercise of power—most crassly, a bump or plug. One sees this happening still more baldly when it comes to younger poets desperate to be affiliated with the avant-garde: one of the most recent above/ground chapbooks I received as of this writing, by someone pseudonymously (I hope) named Baron Rocco Fleetcrest-Seacobs, features anagrammatic poems based on the names of poets, almost all of whom are regularly identified as fixtures in the Canadian avant-garde. "I Ban This Rock", written for Christian Bök, begins

> I is backthorn
> Orbit-ash, nick
> It, chaos brink
> To chain brisk
> Ash into brick,
> I as thickborn
> Oathcrib skin
>
> Inhabits rock,

and continues in this vein for nearly a page.

While this kind of writing calls itself experimental, the conceit is not only paper thin but entirely traditional. It's an exercise that's more predictable and less innovative than even the most hackneyed confessional work from a first-time poet at an open mic who—you guessed it—poured their heart out onto a napkin five minutes before. What's to be gained by writing, or reading, such a poem? The "Baron" states in his mock-archaic page-plus of notes that his bill bissett anagram was "written for and performed at the St. Catharines node" of that poet's 80th birthday celebrations. Gregory Betts, poet and tenured professor at Brock University, also located in St. Catharines, just so happens to get two such anagrammatic honours in the Baron's chapbook. Which at least provides a practical answer to the question of what this stuff is supposed to be doing.[3]

---

3   The Baron's curation of his avant persona continued with an interview, under the author's real name, that appeared on mclennan's blog in February 2021. His commitment to avant tradition here renders even the stilted format of the email interview somehow more artificial, employing as part of

Still, while Fawcett, and any reasonable person, might criticize these socially determined (another word for it would be obsequious) practices of affiliation, inclusion, and exclusion as cynicism, this unprecedented focus on the arbitrariness of the social, extended to create (or foreclose) entire paratextual machineries that are more important than any central text, is more radical than any strict ideology of form or politics of identity due to its exaltation of the individual as an unpredictable social agent—uniquely able to interrupt the academy's totalizing recuperation and commodification of margins.

Just as Kaur's unfeigned inclusivity is radical in its foregrounding of contemporary poetry's ability to be inviting even as it maintains an insider-outsider dynamic, then so is the contemporary avant-garde's contingent cliquishness potentially disruptive of its own elitism—as long as it doesn't get in the habit of doing so. The avant-garde's radical contingency, potentially interruptive as it is, maintains itself as a closed system in the same way as Kaur's seemingly simple lyricism is at once unappealing and inviting. The two fit together in a paradox that would be self-defeating except for the fact that each does the work of making clear to us just how discomforting that work of disruption needs to be.

---

its answers familiar avant, scholarly, and Language Writing tropes to such a degree that the "speaker" emerges as a studied composite of convention. Lines like "Poetry is where I went to break (not just the sense of leisure, but also in the sense of fouling apart; of cracking oneself open and, halfdying, reveling in the starsplint shards)" make one wonder what is experimental, or at all unfamiliar, about such a poetics-cum-persona.

What Were Lyrics?

Near the beginning of my PhD, in 2013, I got into Danish barely-out-of-their-teen-years punk sensations Iceage. They matured beyond a hybrid hardcore/post-punk aesthetic before I did; by the time they released *Plowing into the Field of Love* in 2014, the shambling, two-minutes-or-less scream-eruptions were gone, exchanged for what they thought was a suave, vaguely genderfluid Nick Cave shtick that failed to strike me as either transgressive or appealing. I wanted a more genuinely juvenilized kind of rage, so I tried getting into what were marketed as the realer (code for "younger") Iceage disciples, Lower, only to watch their even more rapid shift from bonkers testosterone minimalism to Cave-esque dramatic monologue. White-guy elocution—isn't this the worst of classic rock? With the narrative of the singer-character (equivalent to the "speaker" that haunts much literary criticism on lyric poetry) driving everything while the band—the non-mouth sound makers—floats in disconnected nothingness behind them? I always wanted to like classic rock and people like Nick Drake. The problem, however, was not only that I couldn't tell the artists apart, but that I couldn't really tell the difference between what I heard and a random loud guy standing on his lawn in the days leading up to Halloween, making sounds about whatever as the pile of leaves he'd just raked up rustled lightly to his front and left.

For the poetry audience out there, does this performance demographic sound familiar? We're in the land of bad lyric poetry, the spectre of which has haunted several essays in this book. Poetry with the voice, the strong feelings, the confession; but where is the sound, the life, the beef? Following up on such a search would bring us to more rhythmic poetry, whether that be Starnino et al's acoustically oriented strains of traditionalist writing, or sonically conversant writing that's nevertheless categorized as conceptualist, or performance-based genres like slam poetry. Whichever you prefer, this is poetry that people not infrequently describe or refer to as music. Like music, there's sound organized according to identifiable rhythmic patterns. Returning to popular music, whether vocals are involved or whether they're a secondary element informing the action, that musical action has to be there. At least as far as I hear things, it's not there in the Doobie Brothers, Nick Cave, later Ice Age, or Lower. And it *needs* to be in poetry, at least in that of the ostensibly embodied, individualistic, lyric sort.

When the 2016 Nobel Prize in Literature went to Bob Dylan, another musician I never exactly fell in love with, the discourse included abundant yet oddly half-hearted debate about the merits and perils of reading pop lyrics as poetry. The semi-agreement that emerged seemed to accept that the two are different but that Dylan's lyrics are complex enough to warrant literary praise. *New Yorker* editor David Remnick perhaps best embodied this consensus when he wrote on 13 Oct. 2016, in a piece entitled "Let's Celebrate the Bob Dylan Nobel Win", "And please: let's not torture ourselves with any gyrations about genre and the holy notion of literature to justify the choice of Dylan", an entity he subsequently describes as "one of the best among us". Which is to say that, Dylan being Dylan, one mustn't quibble about whether his words could be anything but the gold standard of, uh, words.

Similarly, some recent critical works have compared lyrics and literature while largely (and often apologetically) retaining a cautious division between the two. The essays in Michael Robbins' 2017 *Equipment for Living: On Poetry and Pop Music* wistfully articulate the subjective, fleeting, inevitably age-dependent enthusiasm for pop music. Robbins frequently mocks the vapidity of the lyrics themselves, commenting on metalcore band Converge's track "Empty on the Inside", "as opposed to being empty on, like, the outside?"; his framework relies on Kenneth Burke's *The Philosophy of Literary Form* (1974) to argue only for a common "structural assertion" that summons the audience for each medium as a distinct public.

Relatedly, Marxian critic Mark Greif's 2005 essay, "Radiohead, or the Philosophy of Pop", is at pains to find value in the lyrics of one artist even as it dismisses "bad critics" who "show their ignorance when they persist in treating pop like poetry, as in the still-growing critical effluence around Bob Dylan". Most of the music-related essays in Greif's *Against Everything* focus instead on larger historical distinctions between and movements in socially coded genres of popular music. In "Learning to Rap", he laments his adolescent self's obsession with post-punk ("a minor tributary ... of a minor genre [punk]" that was squeezing "the rind of a major genre, rock, that had been basically exhausted by 1972"), which contributed to his missing out on hip hop's "new world-historical form". (He argues something else by the end of the Radiohead essay, but, as I'll discuss shortly, that one's an even bigger copout.)

Maybe we can grapple with this persistent failure to compare pop and poetry, as well as critics' sporadic insistence on the importance of doing so, by looking (again) to Zapruder's *Why Poetry*. Zapruder emphasizes the subjective and non-rational qualities of poetry to make it easier to consume, expanding Keats' Negative Capability to account for the literal, unexplainable, or sensual pleasures of a poem—or, "an intermediate, contradictory state of half knowledge", "where one goes in order to write poetry, and when one reads it". In discussing this central dynamic of reading poetry, and of quantifying the affective, instinctive, or non-rational pleasures associated with the form, Zapruder inadvertently provides a compelling foundation for the reading of pop-rock lyrics as poetry; one that, I think, goes beyond the attempts I've mentioned.

But first, to define my terms. Why the odd, outdated "pop-rock"? Because lyrics aren't the same in lots of genres of popular music. Perhaps most obviously, in the broadly conceived constellation of rap, hip-hop, and related subgenres, lyrics carry an incredible amount of weight. There are just a lot more of them than in the music Robbins, Greif and I discuss, but they're also strikingly more like poetry as we conceive of it on the page. The next exception that comes to mind—and one that admittedly complicates my use of Dylan's literary prominence as an access point to this conversation—is folk. Although it's a genre that never interested me much, folk seems to me to care a lot more than rocklike genres about the story being told and the way it builds or changes as it plods on through the refrain's plot point or lesson. My understanding of folk, with its explicit focus on lyrical content, puts it closer in my taxonomy to the subgenres that make up rap and hip hop, with the latter being quite distant from the cluster of things I'm talking about by privileging not only lyrical content but also the sonics—rhyme, meter, consonance—that themselves define poetry. Perhaps some strains of so-called underground music get closer to poetry without being either hip-hop or folk-adjacent—what I'm thinking of here is the rambling slacker-rock of Pavement and its disciples, or the pieces involving spoken word performances that crop up in the more abstract moments one finds in Xiu Xiu or Posh Isolation's roster. But these moments are contained in larger swaths of lyric practices that hew closer to the simple rhythmic utterances that still provide the bulk of the vocal effects in the wide diffusion of rock-based subgenres. However unpopular my last few examples, I still prefer the archaic *pop* prefix, *pop-rock* recalling as well its straightforward signification at the HMV I frequented as a teenager.

Zapruder goes further than Robbins' emphasis on youth, novelty, and subjectivity because, given the mass-appeal of pop-rock and its function within the (however outdated) conception of "mainstream" Anglophone societies in the West, Zapruder's take on the shortcomings of the closest thing we have to poetry merchants with a captive audience—high-school English teachers—may be relevant to investigations of meaning and (pop-rock) lyric. I draw on some passages from Zapruder's book when I teach poetry to first-year undergraduates, and its proven utility for me in this context establishes its relevance to music. Inevitably in such classes, there are some who hate or "don't get" poetry, and this seems to be part of Zapruder's intended audience, as when he advises, "Despite what you might have heard in school, with certain very limited exceptions, poets do not generally deliberately hide meaning, or write one word and really mean another". Yet the high-school notion of poetry persists. Zapruder goes on:

> In this version of poetry, poems are designed to communicate messages, albeit in a confusing way. Everything that is in the poem—metaphors, similes, imagery, sounds, line breaks, and so on—is decorative, that is, placed on top of the message or meaning of the poem. The student's job is to discover that meaning, and to repeat the central (often banal) message or theme back to the teacher, or in the exam. Bonus points are given for showing how poetic elements enhance this message.

So continues his explication of the wrong way to read poetry, which is meant to resonate with disinterested readers. That is to say, people who just don't get it; those experiencing an absence of knowing that isn't too different from what happens when anyone paying too much attention balks at the "meaning" of song lyrics like "empty on the inside".

This recognition of unmeaning penetrates deeper into the issues than does Greif's one attempt to find social, historical, and political meaning in a specific pop-rock lyric. In "Radiohead, or the Philosophy of Pop", after dismissing the "bad critics" who fixate on Dylan's lyrics, Greif hazards a reading of lyrics by his favourite band, Radiohead. The essay prints in block quotations words from several of the band's "mature" songs, but most notably from the hit-single "Karma Police". This section of the essay includes vapid swaths like "Such a pretty house / and such a pretty garden. / No alarms and no surprises, / no alarms and no surprises, / no alarms and no surprises please"; "This is what you get / this is what you get / this is what you get / when you mess with us"; and "For a minute there / I lost myself, I lost myself. // I'm not here. This isn't happening".

Greif states that such passages are "banal on the page", but then argues that this banality itself registers the "unending low-level fear" characterizing life under neoliberalism. It's a nice trick, and it's very similar to the one we see in some insider praise of the Kootenay School of Writing: the lyrics don't merely show us fear, but instead *really really* show us fear by existing themselves as pure fear. It's the kind of argument that's ultimately subjective but also just too credulous: Greif suggests too that Radiohead somehow anticipates and forecloses questions about the very meaning of song lyrics, the interplay between lyrics and music, *and* the ability of pop music to carry any larger intellectual significance, all because the band is "more able, at the turn of the millennium, to pose a single question: How should it really ever be possible for pop music to incarnate a particular historical situation?". He concludes by doubling down on this construction, arguing that "Radiohead's songs suggest that you should erect a barrier, even of repeated minimal words, or the assertion of a 'we', to protect yourself—and then there proves to be a place in each song to which you, too, can't be admitted, because the singer has something within him closed to interference". Finally, he extends this idea to suggest that the banality of the band's lyrics somehow indicates that "The politics of the next age, if we are to survive, will include a politics of the re-creation of privacy". I'm not convinced. Perhaps Radiohead happens to pull off a masterstroke of linking the plainness of pop-rock lyrics with some larger neoliberal context in this one track, or album, or swath of albums, but the group's supposed genius or singularity (which post-Grade Twelve me also doesn't accept) doesn't explain generations of similarly banal pop-rock lyrics—a banality that doesn't seem to change much, regardless of the political allegiances or purported non-musical intelligence of its practitioners.

Zapruder, on the other hand, engages directly with the at-times surface-level significance of even some of the most revered (and researched) Anglophone poetry. His rejection of the idea that poetry has a hidden meaning urges readers to instead find their reward by "reading what is actually on the page carefully, and allowing one's imagination to adjust to the strangeness of what is there". Accordingly, the tendency not to make any grand conclusions about the comparability of lyrics and poetry probably owes to a broader failure to apply Zapruder's populist advice to pop-rock, that most populist of genres. Drawing on Helen Vendler's ideas about the "aesthetic signature" deriving from lyric poetry's paradoxical evasion and invocation of the unified speaker-author, I think that, in addition to leaving vague or vapid content open to subjective interpretation by an implied audience, pop-rock lyrics often generate an aesthetic signature that emerges almost solely from a vocalist's identifiable rhythmic and sonic qualities, with the latter in many cases existing entirely independently of what would traditionally be described as a song's lyric content.

To better situate, or clarify, what I'm talking about, I want to turn to a brief rejoinder that Greif makes in "Learning to Rap". Late in this essay, he admits,

> I've met real fans of pop music who tell me that they honestly never listen to the lyrics, and don't hear them. This is an entirely different phenomenon, which I respect, though it seems to me a bit like the fact that some people don't dream, or that I'm color-blind to some shades of pink and green—a loss. Anyway, it leads to a different conversation, about timbres and rhythms.

When I read this passage, I wanted to respond in a few ways: first, yes, I want to have that conversation; second, I'm not convinced it is a different conversation, at least when I'm reading Greif's essays in comparison with Robbins' and Zapruder's; third, if it really is a different conversation, I think that difference maps roughly onto a generic difference—that is, the lyric content of hip-hop versus the lyric content of the pop-rock with which Robbins is obsessed, which Greif alternately dismisses (notwithstanding his statements about Dylan and his embrace of hip-hop's world-historical importance) and yet tries to rehabilitate (in his discussion of Radiohead), and which Zapruder's embrace of uncertainty, non-rationality, affect, and unknowability offers some insight into.

What Words Are We Hearing?

If my interest seems frivolous, we can perhaps relate it to the political *dis*engagement operative in mainstream-ish pop-rock as opposed to the more politicized, activist-centered, arguably revolutionary implications of hip hop as Greif conceives of it. But I think it's still worth dwelling on what, exactly, those lyrics are doing—not on the level of political change, but just in terms of the literal, words-on-a-page value Zapruder so compellingly finds at the centre of our poetry-reading practices. And if that value is really so disconnected from what we might call the literary or the political, what does that say about the so-called content of pop lyrics that are considered poetic enough to merit a Nobel Prize in Literature?

I first presented these ideas at a conference in 2018. My method of testing out these hypotheses involved scrolling through the lyrics of Radiohead's "How to Disappear Completely" as the song played for the audience. During instrumental parts I made some haphazard interpretations of the lyrics, following in the vein of Greif's analysis of "Karma Police". In case my expertise in doing so would be called into question, I mentioned my academic credentials and made brief reference to my scattered experiences as a musician.

Around this time, and before I launched into some further poetic analysis, the lyrics printed on the PowerPoint began to include snippets from different Radiohead songs, the pacing of which seemed to fit in with Thom Yorke's drawl as it came from the speakers. Inserted subsequently at various points were lines from goth band Bauhaus' "In the Flat Field" (1980), a theatrical take on late-70s post-punk that has absolutely nothing in common with the Radiohead tracks in question.

So it wasn't *exactly* airtight methodologically... but the people in the room, including a few self-professed lifelong Radiohead fans, seemed not to notice when things went awry on the screen. And some people seemed to have a laugh when I confessed to the stunt, played part of the Bauhaus track, and included a complete swath of Peter Murphy's lyrics that were anything but "banal on the page":

> A gut pull drag on me
> Into the chasm gaping we
> Mirrors multy reflecting this
> Between spunk-stained sheet
> And odorous whim
> Camera eye-flick-shudder within
> Assist me to walk away in sin
> Where is the string that Theseus laid
> Find me out this labyrinth place.

I do get bored, I get bored
In the flat field.
I get bored, I do get bored
In the flat field

The experiment also proved the point made by Andrew Brooks, as part of *The Town Crier*'s series on music and poetry, that the music behind lyrics is not only an "emotional point of entry" to a song, but in fact what carries part of the interpretive weight of those lyrics. Referring to the practice of changing from minor to major key (or vice versa) and the way this alters our perception of what a song "means", Brooks identifies just how much depends on the non-verbal qualities of a song. The drifting malaise of Radiohead, superimposed on either their own lyric banality or Murphy's bluster, gave people pretty much exactly what they expected.

Rhythm and Knowledge

If they're really this interchangeable, what even are lyrics? What do they do? To answer this question in the spirit of Greif, I'll draw on an objective and systematically chosen example: my sometimes-favourite band, the Fall. The group's singer and only constant member (there are 75 or 80 former members), Mark E. Smith, died in January of 2018. Smith has consistently been described as one of the world's most unbearable people. Despite his four decades and dozens of albums worth of music, influence that has been compared to that of David Bowie, and his passing mere days before the 2018 Grammy Awards, the Grammys refused to include his name in their "musicians we've lost" list. *Pitchfork*'s early praise was a couple of days later balanced by a piece called "The Ugly Truths of Loving the Fall's Mark E. Smith", which stated that liking the band required acknowledging that its leader was "a petty, controlling man with significant substance abuse issues that heightened his most malevolent tendencies and often manifested via verbal and physical violence towards those closest to him". In addition to Smith's constant verbal and psychological abuse of anyone who came in contact with him, the band's shows frequently included violence between band members as well as the audience, especially during their early tours of YMCA and Working Men's Clubs (and those during their later meltdown periods).

And yet, this may not have been a case of Iago-like evil, or even a result of Smith's being one of those uniquely irritable and difficult personalities many of us are conditioned to believe are the only kind of people who can make it in the arts. Accounts by Smith's former band members, almost all of whom were tracked down and interviewed by journalist Dave Simpson in his book *The Fallen* (2008), include reports that, by the time he was thirty, Smith's daily regimen included downing a bottle of whisky before three in the afternoon; he was also an avid user of amphetamines and cocaine (although he fired anyone caught using heroin, and many lyrics refer to his hatred of junkies). Erstwhile member Dave Tucker claimed in an interview with Simpson that during his time in the band he never saw Smith eat: "I never saw him put anything in his mouth that didn't have a filter tip or roach attached to it". While it certainly takes a unique constitution to keep up this kind of routine, a big part of what defined Smith was addiction and mental illness.

Smith's vocal style has often been described as manic and agitated. Or, in a particularly literal description often attributed to critic Simon Reynolds, as "a kind of Northern English magic realism that mixed industrial grime with the unearthly and uncanny, voiced through a unique, one-note delivery somewhere between amphetamine-spiked rant and alcohol-addled yarn".

Another notable aspect of Smith's delivery is his weird tendency to tack a dead, unstressed nonsense syllable on the end of phrases that end iambically ("the working class-uh"), giving the impression that sheer force of will, or an amphetamine high, is toggling his English from iambic to trochaic. The content of his lyrics, frequently described as esoteric and wordy, often patched together from working-class Northern Englishisms, would nevertheless register to most listeners as barely comprehensible blather. Then again, a particularly thrilling Fall moment for me comes a little over a minute into the live version of "English Scheme" found on *Fall in a Hole* (1983), when Smith forgets his own lyrics and just adds raw stressed syllables—which the audience enthusiastically and confusedly recreates, likely because some of them are right there in the zone with him and because even those who are familiar with his work have no idea what he was supposed to be saying in the first place. It's a moment that inverts Nicholas Brown's assertion, in his reading of the The White Stripes' album *De Stijl* as a framing exercise, that music that accompanies lyrics inevitably provides "bodily amplification" to verbally expressed sentiment. For Smith, enunciation itself sometimes seems sentiment enough. The effect also seems to bear out Jonathan Culler's recurring emphasis in *Theory of the Lyric* (2015) on the "seductive power of rhythm", which he articulates at one point as a raw "force" that traditional content-and-form interpretations seek to intellectualize or even suppress. Except that even the baseline content-level coherence that's required for poetry to function doesn't really need to be there in the world of pop lyrics.

So maybe the power of the Fall derives from the fact that any part of Mark E. Smith's better-known compositions can be forgotten and seamlessly swapped out for the caveman grunts of caricatured working-class fans (and probably the din of their naysayers). Or, as Remnick's *New Yorker* acknowledged upon Smith's death via its social-media feed, that "Smith's contribution to rock lyrics has been to liberate them from the need to make sense, continuing Captain Beefheart's work".[1] Perhaps negative capability in this context refers more precisely to pop-rock lyrics' role as viscerally rhythmic accompaniment and aesthetic signature—in this case, that of a persona as caustic, criticized, and ravaged as it's been sensationalized. It's not an oversight that this essay hasn't printed any of Smith's lyrics: I don't want anyone to encounter them here, banal and lifeless on the page as they'd be.

---

1   The quote is from an article by Sasha Frere-Jones dating from 2011.

Concluding Precariously

Measures of Astonishment, the collection of the League of Canadian Poets' Anne Szumigalski Lectures, is about what one would expect from an officially sanctioned collection of celebrated poets discussing the power of poetry. It's at once almost spiritual in its enthusiasms but ultimately quaint, with many of the contributors discussing how they came to poetry, why it endures for them, and, of course, the ineffable appeal of the lyric voice. At a few points, it aims for the stars. One equally ambitious and interesting contribution is Margaret Atwood's, which was presented in 2006 and, in being titled "Why Poetry?" is but one short step behind Zapruder's questionless question. The lecture merges Atwood's interests in sci-fi and fantasy with the fundamentals of the form with which she began building her formidable reputation.

Atwood discusses the irrationally (and yet universally) absolute nature of desire: "We know what should be in Heaven: everything we want, and everyone we love. We know what should be in Hell: everything we don't want, and everyone we hate". Her examples become more childish:

> We want to have a large number of sexually attractive partners. We want those we love to love us in return, and to be sexually loyal to us. (Do the math on these two conflicting desires. You won't get even scores.) We want cute, smart children who will treat us with the respect we deserve, and who will not die young or become drug addicts or smash up the car. We want to

157

be surrounded by music, and by ravishing scents and attractive visual objects. We don't want to be too hot. We don't want to be too cold. We want to dance. We want to drink a lot without having a hangover. We want to speak with the animals. We want to be envied. We want to be as gods.

We want wisdom. We want hope. We want to be good. Therefore we sometimes tell ourselves warning stories that deal with the darker side of some of our other wants.

Atwood then pivots to making a practical argument about the value of imagination and creation in any viable system of education. Her feel-good statement that the arts are "not a frill" but "the heart of the matter, because they are about our hearts, and our technological inventiveness is generated by our emotions, not by our minds" resembles those least convincing pro-Humanities arguments. You know the kind. I'm thinking of an especially tiresome meme that goes something like, "Scientists can teach us how to clone dinosaurs, but they lack the infinite ethical wisdom required to tell us that this is a bad idea". (The logic being that Poetry MFAs, unlike those unthinkingly robotic scientists, possess this wisdom in abundance.)

The real value comes with Atwood's statement that we humans are "next door to being in control of everything except earthquakes and the weather"; for this reason, poetry, being "an uttering, our outering, of the human imagination",

lets the shadowy forms of thought and feeling out into the light, where we can take a good look at them and perhaps come to a better understanding of who we are and what we want, and what the limits to those wants may be. Understanding the imagination is not a pastime or even a duty, but a necessity; because increasingly, if we can imagine it, we'll be able to do it.

Poets are not "leftovers from a more archaic age", Atwood concludes, because the absurdity of poetry matches the limitlessness of invention in its real-world, technological sense. While those MFAs might not have much to offer on the question of cloning a dinosaur, their toiling is a type of work that isn't quite experienced by people with the knowledge, skill set, and constitution required to figure out how to clone things, replicate food, print organs and guns, or whatever.

The boring backstory underpinning my own attempt at affirming poetry has in recent months brought me to a similar set of elemental quandaries. I stopped bothering with creative writing when I was pursuing a master's and then doctoral degree in English. A year or two into my PhD, poems started coming again—new ones, new ideas for old ones. I started submitting to journals in a more serious way, and a small percentage were accepted for publication. A few years back I had a poem included in the *Best Canadian Poetry* series. I was surprised that particular poem had resonated with anyone. While Poems.doc (this was for a time the real file name) is so long that Word bounces me back up to the top a few times as I scroll toward the end, I haven't exactly been a prodigious achiever in this area.

I do most of my poetry writing and revising in the procrastination spaces between things like grading papers and doing a fifth round of revisions on a would-be scholarly article. One reason for this compulsive turning away from "actual" work and toward poems is the doubts I've long had about literary criticism—its frequent obscurity, gimmickry, or intellectual dishonesty. Maybe I'm naïve, or just tend to succeed at things that don't make money, but, compared to much literary scholarship, contemporary iterations of which often seem to take a *My argument is that X is an exciting new area of study*, sales-pitch approach, even the most hackneyed lyric poem or redundant found-text exercise has come to seem to me like an idiosyncratic masterstroke. Whatever my misgivings about academia, writing about literature, and poetry in particular, gives you a certain flexibility; the energy required to do its generative (if not really "creative") writing tasks can unexpectedly spin off into poetry ideas and edits that can be attended to at any point of the workday. As a lot of us are aware, there are many, many other ways of struggling to earn a living that don't permit this kind of practice.

Another thing that's kept Poems.doc open is the uncertainty faced by so many people in my situation. Precarity instills a dread in everyone save the most overconfident gimmick-artists that each semester could be the last time we'll work in the field we've trained in for years. For me, this financial uncertainty and looming sense of career failure is compounded by the fact that so much of what you produce in this profession—conference presentations, articles, grant proposals, academic book reviews, lecture notes—will end up having been worth essentially nothing the moment you've left the academic ecosystem. At any moment you could become precisely one of those outsiders who is utterly unable (or at least unmotivated) to see any value in the writing that's long been your primary output. Around a year after finishing my PhD, a fortuitous connection gave me the opportunity to stave off this reality for another three years: a brief question to an acquaintance about how they found an academic position overseas led to a medium-term teaching and research opportunity at a university in mainland China.

A little over a year into the contract, I finished up the fall term and went on what was supposed to be a short vacation. This was January 2020, just before the city in which COVID-19 originated— which had been my home for more than a year—locked down and barred me from returning. But before any of that happened, I moved through several countries in Southeast Asia and witnessed a different kind of hopeless, shambolic mass of lost souls. Khaosan Road, the infamous backpacker destination made recognizable by the Leo DiCaprio vehicle *The Beach*, was by day a spectacle much more horrific than that depicted in the film. Long swaths of the smaller streets fanning out from the main thoroughfare featured interchangeable lounge-style restaurants and bars, seats on either side turned toward the stream of (mostly Western) tourists flowing down the road in their backpacking outfits, anachronistic downtempo pumping over the speakers as the veteran expats cast silent, gladiatorial judgment on the travelers and newcomers. The scene made me think of a book I'd just finished reading: Daniel Immerwahr's *How to Hide an Empire: A History of the Greater United States* (2019). Immerwahr compellingly articulates the way hybrid artistic and social formations arose from the presence of overseas military bases during and after the Second World War, resulting in everything from Sony's portable radios to the Beatles. From a post-COVID viewpoint, my meandering professional-creative path had taken me through what might prove to have been the final moments of American culture's steady expansion into overseas markets.

The positive image I've tried to create in these pages—of a heterogeneous, shifting, and yet unified non-economy of multivalent work—and through which the above journey took place, could be adjusted to reflect instead the Khaosan where it ended up: a clutter of curios, or just tchotchkes, produced and consumed by insiders and by outsiders redefining themselves amid shifting cultural detritus in an apocalyptic game of musical chairs. This alternate landscape brings to mind Joyelle McSweeney's idea of the Loser Occult, articulated near the end of *The Necropastoral: Poetry, Media, Occults* (2015) as a parallel world of unliving connections and resonances in which are reflected the decay and degradation that define our historical moment. The section, which begins by referring to an "I miss Ronald Reagan" bumper sticker, defines the Loser Occult as "a rejection of any concept of literature still trying to worship at that old altar of patrilineage, of literary inheritance". McSweeney continues,

> The loser occult knocks that edifice down, hangs out in the rubble huffing, hallucinating, gossiping, making out, wasting time, confecting new and obscene humanoid and nonhumanoid forms. Loser occult envisions a kind of leveled, ambivalent, invisible perpetuity without precedence or antecedence, not based on permanence but on decay, infloration, contamination. It rejects youth, youthful promise, power, vigor, resonance, and shared experience but allows for the possibility of weird mutation, arbitrary reanimation, coincidence, corrosion, drag, and psychic twinship.

Like Khaosan, McSweeney's take is quintessentially American—in its array of kitschy pop-culture detritus, but also in the way that the necro-spectacle envisions even perpetual decay as within the limits of an immutable condition of boredom and disposable income. In other words, of unending luxury.

Immerwahr's book stayed with me after I realized a return to China wasn't viable and found myself waiting out travel restrictions in the Philippines for a few weeks, surrounded by the jeepneys I had read about in its pages. Yet, whereas Immerwahr writes of the fruitful collision of loser cultures—American GIs and the local populations that felt compelled to adapt their own cultural practices to meet the market needs of the former—the Khaosan Road I saw struck me as an unfortunate, downtempo-obsessed outgrowth of this, where not the locals but the Westerners try out anachronistic or hybridized variants of Western culture for the first time. Immerwahr writes of a positive dialectical encounter, similar to the one I've found in contemporary poetry culture's ability to make something out of ostensible opposites without transcending those antagonisms. Khaosan Road seemed more like McSweeney's burned-out necropastoral, unliving in the mess of its luxurious decay.

It seems like the capacities for limitless poesis in science and art that Atwood spoke of have been foreclosed by the pandemic, at least for now. Instead, we have a rapidly shifting situation in which it may get harder to tell who the losers are, or what interests are occult. One of the more implicit arguments I've made here is that mainstreaming poetry in any meaningful sense would destroy that dynamic in which an ostensible unproductivity reveals itself as in fact incredibly productive. Poetry remains distinct in its removal from the mainstream and its refraction of the values of the everyday. If the poetry of the past made nothing happen, can the poetry of the future, staring down the combination of socio-economic decline and undifferentiated excess, function as its own economy of meaning? Can a struggle that involves the work of learning and doing make for a more engaged form of post-privilege?

Then again, isn't obsessively producing something without value and without much return just pure neoliberalism—the offloading of economic and systemic failures onto the self-improving, always-producing individual? Isn't perpetual unwaged labour the sinister obverse of the basic-income coin? Maybe. But what are the alternatives? Perhaps staying closer to ourselves, and doing work like the work of poetry—work that sits at the margins between value and meaninglessness, practical good and abstract virtue, in-group and out-group—might give us the tools to orient ourselves, without requiring either a transfer of our energies to boutique activism or an insistence on the poem's unchanging location in some inaccessible literary firmament. Instead of making nothing happen, maybe the work of poetry is one of the few ways in which we can make something out of nothing.

Bibliography

Poetry

Abel, Jordan. *Timeless American Classic.* above/ground Press, 2017.

Anstee, Cameron. *Book of Annotations.* Invisible Press, 2018.

Barger, John Wall. *Dying in Dharamsala.* The Alfred Gustav Press, 2018, Series 19.

Belcourt, Billy-Ray. *NDN Coping Mechanisms.* House of Anansi Press, 2019.

Bök, Christian. *Xenotext.* Coach House Books, 2015.

Casteels, Michael E., and Nicholas Papaxanthos. *All We've Learned, Which Isn't Much.* above/ground Press, 2020.

---. *Lagoon. Still Lagoon.* Puddles of Sky Press, 2017.

Charleston, Cortney Lamar. *Telepathologies.* Saturnalia Books, 2017.

Fleetcrest-Seacobs, Baron Rocco. *Man Agar.* above/ground Press, 2020.

Fleming, Ally. *The Worst Season.* Anstruther Press, 2017.

Giovannone, Aaron. *The Nonnets.* Book*hug Press, 2018.

Hajnoczky, Helen. *Magyarázni.* Coach House Books, 2016.

---. *No Right on Red.* above/ground Press, 2017.

---. *Other Observations.* ?! Press, 2018.

---. *Variations on the Stillness of Motion.* ?! Press, 2018.

Kaur, Rupi. *Home Body.* Andrews McMeel Publishing, 2020.

---. *Milk and Honey.* Andrews McMeel Publishing, 2014.

---. *The Sun and Her Flowers.* Andrew McMeel Publishing, 2017.

Liem, Tess. *Tell everybody I say hi.* Anstruther Press, 2017.

MacEwen, Gwendolyn. "Dark Pines Under Water." *The Shadow-Maker*, Macmillan, 1969, p. 50.

Purdy, Al. "Piling Blood." 1984. *Rooms for Rent in the Outer Planets: Selected Poems 1962-1996*, edited by Sam Solecki, Harbour Publishing, 1996, pp. 110-12.

Queyras, Sina. *Expressway*. Coach House, 2009.

Radmore, Claudia Coutu. *On Fogo*. The Alfred Gustav Press, 2018. Series 19.

Starnino, Carmine. "San Pellegrino." *Leviathan*, Coach House Books, 2016. *The Walrus*, 8 July 2016, https://thewalrus.ca/san-pellegrino/.

Surani, Moez. *Are the Rivers in Your Poems Real*. Book*hug Press, 2019.

---. عملية *Operación Opération Operation* 行动 Операция. Book*hug Press, 2016.

Thammavongsa, Souvankham. *Light*. Pedlar Press, 2013.

---. *Small Arguments*. Pedlar Press, 2003.

Thornton, Russell. *Aftermath*. The Alfred Gustav Press, 2018. Series 19.

Trussler, Michael. *Light's Alibi*. The Alfred Gustav Press, 2018. Series 19.

Verboom, Andy. *Orthric Sonnets*. Baseline Press, 2017.

Wayman, Tom. *Free Time: Industrial Poems*. Macmillan, 1977.

Wreggitt, Andrew. *Riding to Nicola Country*. Harbour Publishing, 1981.

---. *Man at Stellaco River*. Thistledown Press, 1984.

---. "On Wasting Time." *Storm Warning 2: The New Canadian Poets*, edited by Al Purdy, McClelland and Stewart, 1976, pp. 150-51.

Wright, Catriona. *Table Manners*. Signal Editions, 2017.

Secondary Sources

Abel, Jordan. *Injun*. above/ground Press, 2016.

---. *The Place of Scraps*. above/ground Press, 2013.

---. *Un/inhabited*. above/ground Press, 2014.

Abley, Mark. "The Angel of the Big Muddy." *Measures of Astonishment: Poets on Poetry*, presented by the League of Canadian Poets, University of Regina Press, 2016, pp. 79-98.

Aesop. *Fables*, translated by George Fyler Townsend, EPUB edition.

Anstee, Cameron. *Words in Place*. Puddles of Sky Press, 2021.

Appiah, Kwame Anthony. *The Lies That Bind: Rethinking Identity: Creed, Country, Color, Class, Culture*. LiveRight, 2018.

Atwood, Margaret. "Why Poetry?" *Measures of Astonishment: Poets on Poetry*, presented by the League of Canadian Poets, University of Regina Press, 2016, pp. 69-77.

Ball, Jonathan. "Pop Culture, Nostalgia Shimmer in Verse." Review of Nathan Dueck, *A Very Special Episode*, Moez Surani, *Are the Rivers in Your Poems Real*, Howard White, *A Mysterious Humming Noise*, Ben Ladouceur, Mad Long Emotion. *Winnipeg Free Press*, 28 December 2019, https://www.winnipegfreepress.com/arts-and-life/entertainment/books/pop-culture-nostalgia-shimmer-in-verse-566532902.html.

Balzer, David. *Curationism: How Curating Took Over the Art World and Everything Else.* Coach House Books, 2014.

Barton, John. "Approaching Utopia: The Poetries of Billy-Ray Belcourt and Ben Ladouceur." *We Are Not Avatars: Essays, Memoirs, Manifestos*, Palimpsest, 2019, pp. 94-116.

Bataille, Georges. "The Notion of Expenditure." *Visions of Excess: Selected Writings, 1927-1939*, edited by Allan Stoekl, translated by Allan Stoekl with Carl R. Lovitt and Donald. M. Leslie, Jr., University of Minnesota Press, 1985, pp. 116-129.

Battan, Carrie. "Vampire Weekend's Ezra Koenig Defends Selfies." *Pitchfork*, 22 Nov. 2013. *Echo Chamber*, https://pitchfork.com/news/53107-echo-chamber-vampire-weekends-ezra-koenig-defends-selfies/.

Bayot, David Jonathan. Preface. *Circling the Canon: The Selected Book Reviews of Marjorie Perloff, 1969-1994*, vol. 1., edited by Bayot, University of New Mexico Press, 2019, pp. ix-xiv.

Beaulieu, Derek Alexander. *Seen of the Crime: Essays on Conceptual Writing.* Snare Books, 2011.

Bennett, Andrea. "Another Battle in Service of the War: Donato Mancini's *You Must Work Harder to Write the [sic] Poetry of Excellence*." *Arc*, 4 July 2013, https://arcpoetry.ca/2013/07/04/another-battle-in-service-of-the-war-donato-mancinis-you-must-work-harder-to-write-the-poetry-of-excellence/.

Berardi, Franco "Bifo." *Breathing: Chaos and Poetry.* Semiotext(e), 2018. Intervention Series.

Bernstein, Charles. "Poetry Scene Investigation: A Conversation with Marjorie Perloff." *Attack of the Difficult Poems*, University of Chicago Press, 2011, pp. 239-55.

---. "Provisional Institutions: Alternative Presses and Poetic Innovation." *My Way: Speeches and Poems*, University of Chicago Press, 1999, pp. 145-54.

Bernstein, Felix. *Notes on Post-Conceptual Poetry.* Insert Blanc Press, 2015.

Betts, Gregory. "Before Our Time: Radical English-Canadian Poetries Across the Post/Modern Divide." *Canadian Poetry*, no. 60, Spring/Summer 2007, pp. 22-45.

Betts, Gregory, and Christian Bök. "Time for the Avant-Garde in Canada." *Avant Canada: Poets, Prophets, Revolutionaries*, edited by Betts and Bök, Wilfrid Laurier University Press, 2019, pp. 3-15.

Bök, Christian. Afterword. *Ground Works: Avant-Garde for Thee*, House of Anansi, 2003, pp. x-y.

---. "Statements." *Experimental Literature: A Collection of Statements*, edited by Jeffrey R. Di Leo and Warren Motte, JEF Books / Depth Charge Publishing, 2018, pp. 63-70.

Boothby, Aaron. "Against Assessment; Please Bring Snacks." *The Town Crier*, 9 Mar. 2020, Comments on Our Review Culture, http://towncrier.puritan-magazine.com/aaron-boothby-against-assessment/.

Bourdieu, Pierre. "The Forms of Capital." *Handbook of Theory and Research for the Sociology of Education*, edited by J. Richardson, Greenwood Publishing, 1986, pp. 241–58.

Bowering, George. "Unexpected Objects." *The Contemporary Canadian Poem Anthology*, vol. 1, Coach House Books, 1983. pp. 1-3.

Brand, Dionne, and Souvankham Thammavongsa. "The Voice Asking." *What the Poets Are Doing: Canadian Poets in Conversation*, edited by Rob Taylor, Nightwood Editions, 2018, pp. 55-68.

Brooks, Andrew. "Major and Minor Points." *The Town Crier,* 23 August 2017, http://towncrier.puritan-magazine.com/songwriter/.

Brown, Nicholas. *Autonomy: The Social Ontology of Art under Capitalism*. Duke University Press, 2019.

Burke, Kenneth. *The Philosophy of Literary Form*. University of California Press, 1974.

Burnham, Clint. *The Only Poetry That Matters: Reading the Kootenay School of Writing*. Arsenal Pulp Press, 2011.

Burt, Stephanie. *Don't Read Poetry*. Basic Books, 2019.

---. *the poem is you*. The Belknap Press of Harvard University Press, 2016.

---. *Close Calls with Nonsense*. Graywolf Press, 2009.

Butling, Pauline, and Susan Rudy. *Writing in Our Time: Canada's Radical Poetries in English   (1957-2003)*. Wilfrid Laurier University Press, 2005.

Chong, Philipa. *Inside the Circle: Book Reviewing in Uncertain Times*. Princeton University Press, 2020.

Clover, Joshua. "The Genealogical Avant-Garde." *Lana Turner Journal*, no. 7, 2015, http://www.lanaturnerjournal.com/7/the-genealogical-avant-garde.

Crosbie, Lynn. Review of *The New Canon: An Anthology of Canadian Poets*, edited by Carmine Starnino. *University of Toronto Quarterly*, vol. 76, no. 1, Winter 2007, pp. 629-30.

Culler, Jonathan. *Theory of the Lyric*. Harvard University Press, 2015.

Daymond, Douglas. "In Minor Key." Review of *Running into the Open*, by Pamela Banting, *Cattail Week*, by Brian Bartlett, *From Here to Here*, by Endre Farkas,

Adam 2000, by Orin Manitt, *A Queen Is Holding a Mummified Cat*, by Mary Melfi, *Signs and Certainties*, by A.F. Moritz, *Finding Mom at Eaton's*, by George Morrissette, *The Space Between Sleep and Waking*, by Robyn Sarah, *The Cost of Living*, by Kenneth Sherman, and *Riding to Nicola Country*, by Andrew Wreggitt. *Canadian Literature*, no. 97, Summer 1983, pp. 140-43.

Deleuze, Gilles, and Félix Guattari. "What Is a Minor Literature?" *Out There: Marginalization and Contemporary Cultures*, edited by Russell Ferguson et al, The MIT Press, 1990, pp. 59-69.

Dewart, Edward Hartley. *Selections from Canadian Poets with Occasional Critical and Biographical Notes and an Introductory Essay on Canadian Poetry*. 1864. University of Toronto Press, 1973.

Di Leo, Jeffrey R., and Warren Motte, editors. *Experimental Literature: A Collection of Statements*. JEF Books/ Depth Charge Publishing, 2018.

Dickinson, Adam. *Kingdom, Phylum*. Brick Books, 2006.

Du Plessis, Klara. "A Cocktail of Criticism: Reconsidering CanLit Review Culture." *The Town Crier*, 5 March 2020. *The Puritan*, http://towncrier. puritan-magazine.com/klara-du-plessis-cocktail-criticism/.

Dworkin, Craig, and Kenneth Goldsmith, editors. *Against Expression: An Anthology of Conceptual Writing*. Northwestern University Press, 2011.

Fawcett, Brian. "East Van Über Alles?" *Unusual Circumstances, Interesting Times and Other Impolite Interventions*, New Star, 1991, pp. 91-102.

Flood, Alison. "Prize-Nominated Poet's Debut Cancelled as Plagiarism Accusations Build." *The Guardian*, 6 December 2018, https://www. theguardian.com/books/2018/dec/06/prize-nominated-poets-debut-cancelled-as-plagiarism-accusations-build.

Frere-Jones, Sasha. "Plug and Play: The Endless Inspiration of the Fall." *The New Yorker*, 7 November 2011, https://www.newyorker.com/ magazine/2011/11/14/plug-and-play/.

Gass, William H. *Reading Rilke: Reflecting on the Problems of Translation*. A. Knopf, 1999.

Glickman, Susan. *The Picturesque and the Sublime: A Poetics of the Canadian Landscape*. McGill-Queen's University Press, 1998.

Greif, Mark. "Radiohead, or the Philosophy of Pop." *Against Everything*, Vintage, 2016, pp. 99-117.

Guriel, Jason. "The Case Against Reading Everything." *The Walrus*, 13 December 2017, https://thewalrus.ca/the-case-against-reading-everything/.

---. "Did You Know You Were a Writer?: Revisiting Roald Dahl's 'Lucky Break.'" *Canadian Notes and Queries*, no. 93, Summer 2015, pp. 16-17.

---. *The Pigheaded Soul: Essays and Reviews on Poetry and Culture*. The Porcupine's Quill, 2013.

Han, Byung-Chul. *The Burnout Society*. Translated by Erik Butler, Stanford University Press, 2015. Stanford Briefs.

Harris, Kaplan. "A Zine Ecology of Charles Bernstein's Selected Poems." *Postmodern Culture: Journal of Interdisciplinary Thought on Contemporary Cultures,* vol. 20, no. 3, May 2010, http://www.pomoculture. org/2013/09/03/a-zine-ecology-of-charles-bernsteins-selected-poems/.

Hodd, Thomas. *#NoMoreNotes*. Anstruther Press, 2016. Manifesto Series 3.

Hunt, Ken. *Manhattan Project*. University of Calgary Press, 2020.

Hutcheon, Linda. *The Canadian Postmodern: A Study of Contemporary English-Canadian Fiction*. Oxford University Press, 1988.

Immerwahr, Daniel. *How to Hide an Empire: A History of the Greater United States*. Farrar, Straus and Giroux, 2019.

Kay, Jonathan. "For Journalists, the New York Times' Social-Justice Meltdown Is a Sign of Things to Come." *Quillette*, 9 June 2020, https://quillette. com/2020/06/09/for-journalists-the-new-york-times-social-justice-meltdown-is-a-sign-of-things-to-come/.

Khaira-Hanks, Priya. "Rupi Kaur: The Inevitable Backlash against Instagram's Favourite Poet." *The Guardian*, 4 October 2017, https://www.theguardian. com/books/booksblog/2017/oct/04/rupi-kaur-instapoets-the-sun-and-her-flowers/.

"Künstlerroman." *Encyclopedia of Literature in Canada*. Edited by William H. New, University of Toronto Press, 2002, p. 596.

Lahey, Ernestine. "'One of us': Purdy, Elite Culture, and the Visual Arts." *An Echo in the Mountains: Al Purdy after a Century*. Edited by Nicholas Bradley, McGill-Queen's University Press, 2020, pp. 218-239.

Lasky, Dorothea, and Alex Dimitrov. *Astro Poets: Your Guides to the Zodiac*. EPUB ed., Flatiron Books, 2019.

Lerner, Ben. *The Hatred of Poetry*. Farrar, Straus and Giroux, 2016.

Lista, Michael. "The Good in Bad Reviews." *National Post*, 29 June 2012, https:// nationalpost.com/afterword/michael-lista-on-poetry-the-good-in-bad-reviews/.

---. "Poetry Slam." *The Walrus*, 13 June 2016, https://thewalrus.ca/poetry-slam/.

---. *Strike Anywhere: Essays, Reviews & Other Arsons*. The Porcupine's Quill, 2016.

Lochhead, Douglas. Introduction. *Selections from Canadian Poets with Occasional Critical and Biographical Notes and an Introductory Essay on Canadian Poetry*, edited by Edwin Hartley Dewart, 1864, University of Toronto Press, 1973.

Mann, Paul. *The Theory-Death of the Avant-Garde*. Indiana University Press, 1991.

Mancini, Donato. *You Must Work Harder to Write Poetry of Excellence: Crafts Discourse and the Common Reader in Canadian Poetry Book Reviews.* Toronto: Book*hug Press, 2012. Department of Critical Thought 7.

mclennan, rob. *Subverting the Lyric: Essays.* ECW Press, 2008.

McQuillan, David. *Aesthetic Scandal and Accessibility: The Subversive Simplicity of Rupi Kaur's* milk and honey. 2018. Dalhousie University, MA thesis. DalSpace, https://dalspace.library.dal.ca/xmlui/bitstream/handle/10222/74202/McQuillan-David-MA-ENGL-August-2018.pdf?sequence=3&isAllowed=y/.

McSweeney, Joyelle. *The Necropastoral: Poetry, Media, Occults.* EPUB ed., University of Michigan Press, 2015. Poets on Poetry.

Middleton, Peter. "The Contemporary Poetry Reading." *Close Listening: Poetry and the Performed Word,* edited by Charles Bernstein, Oxford University Press, 1998, pp. 262-99.

Milne, Heather. "Writing the Body Politic: Feminist Poetics in the Twenty-First Century." *Public Poetics: Critical Issues in Canadian Poetry and Poetics,* edited by Bart Vautour, Erin Wunker, Travis V. Mason, and Christl Verduyn, Wilfrid Laurier University Press, 2012, pp. 65-86.

Motte, Warren F. "Clinamen Redux." *Comparative Literature Studies,* vol. 23, no. 4, Winter 1986, pp. 263-81

Neilson, Shane. "We Shall Know You by Your Reviews: The New White Male and Alden Nowlan's *Collected Poems.*" *The Miramichi Reader,* 30 January 2020, miramichireader.ca.

Ngai, Sianne. *Our Aesthetic Categories: Zany, Cute, Interesting.* Harvard University Press, 2012.

Park Hong, Cathy. "There's a New Movement in American Poetry and It's Not Kenneth Goldsmith." *The New Republic,* 1 October 2015, https://newrepublic.com/article/122985/new-movement-american-poetry-not-kenneth-goldsmith/.

Perloff, Marjorie. *Frank O'Hara: Poet Among Painters.* G. Braziller, 1977.

---. "The French Connection." Review of *The Random House Book of Twentieth-Century French Poetry,* edited by Paul Auster, *A Tomb for Anatole,* by Stephane Mallarmé, *Poems of André Breton,* edited and translated by Jean-Pierre Cauvin and Mary Ann Caws, *The Making of the Pré,* by Francis Ponge, translated by Lee Fahnenstock, and *The Collected Poetry,* by Aimé Césaire. *Circling the Canon: The Selected Book Reviews of Marjorie Perloff, 1969-1994,* vol. 1, edited by David Jonathan Bayot, University of New Mexico Press, pp. 184-205.

---. "Poetry on the Brink: Reinventing the Lyric." *Boston Review,* vol. 37, no. 3, May/June 2012, http://bostonreview.net/archives/BR37.3/marjorie_perloff_poetry_lyric_ reinvention.php/.

---. "Reading Gass Reading Rilke." Review of *Reading Rilke: Reflections on the Problems of Translation*, by William H. Gass. *Circling the Canon*, vol. 2: *The Selected Book Reviews of Marjorie Perloff, 1995-2017*, edited by David Jonathan Bayot, University of New Mexico Press, 2019, pp. 72-89.

---. *Unoriginal Genius: Poetry by Other Means in the New Century*. University of Chicago Press, 2010.

Place, Vanessa, and Robert Fitterman. *Notes on Conceptualisms*. Ugly Duckling Press, 2009.

Poetry Foundation. "Poetry Foundation on COVID-19 Relief." 23 April 2020, https://www.poetryfoundation.org/foundation/press/153378/poetry-foundation-oncovid-19-relief/.

Pool, Gail. *Faint Praise: The Plight of Book Reviewing in America*. University of Missouri Press, 2007.

Queyras, Sina. "Lyric Conceptualism, a Manifesto in Progress." *Harriet*, Poetry Foundation, 9 April 2012, https://www.poetryfoundation.org/harriet/2012/04/lyric-conceptualism-a-manifesto-in-progress/.

Raycroft, Brent. "Who's Afraid of Orpheus and Eurydice?: Christian Bök's *The Xenotext Book 1*." *Arc*, 25 February 2017, https://arcpoetry.ca/2017/02/25/whos-afraid-of-orpheus-and-eurydice-christian-boks-the-xenotext-book-1/.

Reed, Alan. Review of *For Love and Autonomy*, by Anahita Jamali Rad. *Debutantes*, 30 April 2017, https://debutantes.squarespace.com/lessai/2017/4/30/for-love-and-autonomy/.

Reed, Brian M. *Nobody's Business: Twenty-First Century Avant-Garde Poetics*. Cornell University Press, 2013.

Remnick, David. "Let's Celebrate the Bob Dylan Nobel Win." *The New Yorker*, 13 October 2016, https://www.newyorker.com/culture/cultural-comment/lets-celebrate-the-bob-dylan- nobel-win/.

Robbins, Michael. *Equipment for Living: On Poetry and Pop Music*. Simon and Schuster, 2017.

---. "Ripostes." Review of *Postmodern American Poetry: A Norton Anthology*, edited by Paul Hoover. *Poetry*, vol. 202, no. 4, July/August 2013, pp. 387-97.

Roberts, John. *Revolutionary Time and the Avant-Garde*. EPUB ed., Verso, 2015.

Seip, Katye. "Exile and Audience: Carmine Starnino and the Poetics of Engagement." *Canadian Poetry*, no. 64, Spring/Summer 2009, pp. 112-126.

Sennett, Richard. *The Craftsman*. Yale University Press, 2008.

Share, Don. "Poetry Makes Nothing Happen...Or Does It?" *Harriet*, Poetry Foundation, 4 November 2009, https://www.poetryfoundation.org/harriet/2009/11/poetry-makes-nothing-happen-or-does-it/.

Shepard, Jim. "Jim Shepard on Why We Still Need Literary Journals; Thank God for the Small Magazines." *Literary Hub*, 19 September 2019. https://lithub.com/jim-shepard-on-why-we-still-need-literary-jou rnals/?fbclid=IwAR13eriG7GasufkmvzyOJzMwQpzHH1Bn3j903-34Gqybf11O6vgMG-I_GfU/.

Shepherd, Reginald. "Who You Callin' 'Post-Avant'?" *Harriet*, Poetry Foundation, 6 February 2008, https://www.poetryfoundation.org/harriet/2008/02/who-you-callin-post-avant/.

Silverberg, Mark. "The Can(adi)onization of Al Purdy." *Essays on Canadian Writing*, no. 70, Spring 2000, pp. 226-51.

Simpson, Dave. *The Fallen: Life In and Out of Britain's Most Insane Group*. Kindle ed., Canongate, 2009.

Skolnik, Jes. "The Ugly Truths of Loving the Fall's Mark E. Smith." *Pitchfork*, 26 January 2018, https://pitchfork.com/thepitch/the-ugly-truths-of-loving-the-falls-mark-e-smith/.

speCt books. "An Open Letter to the Poetry Foundation Regarding Their COVID-19 Response Statement." *speCt!*, 27 April 2020, http://spectbooks. com/an-open-letter-to-the-poetry-foundation-regarding-their-covid-19-response-statement/.

---. "Tell the Poetry Foundation to be Accountable to its Community." Change.org, 6 June 2020, https://www.change.org/p/writers-ask-the-poetry-foundation-to-support-poets-and-their-allies?recruiter=306385 917&recruited_by_id=8860be00-0567-11e5-b216-819c7b3c9d4e&utm_ source=share_petition&utm_medium=copylink&utm_ campaign=petition_dashboard/.

Starnino, Carmine. "An Interview with Carmine Starnino." Interview by Tim Bowling, *Contemporary Verse 2*, vol. 36, no. 2, Fall 2013, pp. 7–19.

---. Introduction. *The New Canon*, edited by Starnino, Signal, 2005, pp. 15-36.

Sur, Sanchari. "Reviewing with Intention: Negotiating the Ethical Dilemma of a Balanced Review." *The Town Crier*, 19 Mar. 2020, http://towncrier.puritan-magazine.com/sanchari-sur-reviewing-with-intention/.

Surani, Moez. *Cairo*. Left Hand Press, 2009.

---. "The Chat with Moez Surani." Interview by Trevor Corkum, *49th Shelf*, 26 February 2020, https://49thshelf.com/Blog/2020/02/26/The-Chat-with-Moez-Surani/.

---. *Floating Life*. Wolsak and Wynn, 2012.

---. *Reticent Bodies*. Wolsak and Wynn, 2009.

---. *The Viscount's Goats*. Delirium Press, 2004.

Sylvester, Nick. "It's Just a Cassette." *Pitchfork*, 6 September 2013, https:// pitchfork.com/features/oped/9212-its-just-a-cassette/.

Taylor, Rob. "Rob Taylor." *Beyond Forgetting: Celebrating 100 Years of Al Purdy; An Anthology of Poems Written in Tribute to Al Purdy*, edited by Howard White and Emma Skagen, Harbour Publishing, 2018, p. 167.

---. *What the Poets Are Doing: Canadian Poets in Conversation*. Nightwood Editions, 2002.

Thran, Nick. Review of *Eight Track*, by Oana Avasilichioaei, and *Are the Rivers in Your Poems Real*, by Moez Surani. *Event*, vol. 49, no. 1, 27 August 2020, https://www.eventmagazine.ca/2020/08/nick-thran-reviews-491/

Vendler, Helen. Introduction. *Soul Says: On Recent Poetry*, Belknap Press of Harvard University Press, 1995, pp. 1-8.

Voyce, Stephen. *Poetic Community: Avant-Garde Activism and Cold War Culture*. University of Toronto Press, 2013.

Vozick-Levinson, Simon. "Ezra Koenig: Believe in Your Selfie." *Rolling Stone*, 22 November 2013, https://www.rollingstone.com/music/music-news/ezra-koenig-believe-in-your-selfie-191641/.

Wallace, Jade. "USEREVIEW 023 (Capsule): The Knowing Animals." Review of *The Knowing Animals*, by Emily Skov-Nielsen. *Carousel*, 9 March 2021, http://blog.carouselmagazine.ca/usereview023capsule/.

---. "Usereview Editorial." *Carousel*, no. 44, Fall 2020, http://carouselmagazine.ca/c44-usereview-editorial/.

Warner, Michael. *Publics and Counterpublics*. New York: Zone Books, 2005.

Watts, Carl. *Oblique Identity: Form and Whiteness in Recent Canadian Poetry*. Frog Hollow, 2019

Watts, Rebecca. "The Cult of the Noble Amateur." *PN Review* 239, vol. 44, no. 3, January-February 2018, https://www.pnreview.co.uk/cgi-bin/scribe?item_id=10090/.

Wheeler, Lesley. *Voicing American Poetry: Sound and Performance from the 1920s to the Present*. Cornell University Press, 2008.

White, Howard, and Emma Skagen, editors. *Beyond Forgetting: Celebrating 100 Years of Al Purdy; An Anthology of Poems Written in Tribute to Al Purdy*. Harbour Publishing, 2018.

"Why Is Poetry Having a Moment?" *News*, The London School of Economics and Political Science, 13 December 2019, http://www.lse.ac.uk/News/Latest-news-from-LSE/2019/L-December-2019/Why-is-poetry-having-a-moment?utm_source=ImpactNewsletter&utm_medium=email&utm_

Wood, Brent. "From The Rising Fire to Afterworlds: The Visionary Circle in the Poetry of Gwendolyn MacEwen." *Canadian Poetry: Studies, Documents, Reviews*, no. 47, Fall/Winter 2000, pp. 40-69.

Wunker, Erin. "O Little Expressway: Sina Queyras and the Traffic of Subversive Hope." *ESC: English Studies in Canada*, vol. 36, no. 1, March 2010, pp. 37-55.

Zapruder, Matthew. *Why Poetry*. Ecco, 2017.

Zelazo, Suzanne. "Slipping Teeth into Lemon: Reading Sina Queyras Reading." *Beyond Stasis: Feminism and Poetics Today*, special issue of *Open Letter*, Summer 2009, pp. 195-2014.

Zwicky, Jan. "The Ethics of the Negative Review." *The Malahat Review*, no. 144, Fall 2003.

Tweets Cited

Agnew, Marion. @shuniahwriter. "That "I wrote this on the way over" thing! Argh. If you imagine your raw thoughts to be so fascinating, well OK, but don't say so." Replying to @carl_a_watts @mocklerswriting. 5:57 a.m. 8 July 2019.

Astro Poets. @poetastrologers. "Week of 11/29 in Sagittarius: It's time to ask for what you really want. You might not get it, but in the asking you will see what it is. If you can at dawn take note of the way there is always possibility. Wear the air of dreams as close as you can to the throat." 10:51 p.m. 29 Nov. 2020.

Colangelo, Jeremy. @JRColangelo. "Shows up at an open mic with Howl and Other Poems in their pocket: "Alright befor I get to my own stuff, just to mix things up..." Replying to @carl_a_watts @mocklerswriting. 7:57 p.m. 7 July 2019.

Malli, Nisa. @nisamalliwrites. ""I wrote this poem in the cab over / just this morning" Replying to @dean_garlick @mocklerswriting. 5:00 p.m. 7 July 2019.

Mockler's Writing Workshop. @mocklerswriting. "What are some terrible, funny, awkward things poets do at readings? Like read too long, brag too much, etc. Sourcing for a scene I'm writing." 4:51 p.m. 7 July 2019.

Mooney, Jacob McArthur. [right arrow][right arrow]drift anthemic[right arrow][right arrow]   @McArthurMooney. "Every time someone reads something they wrote that day I want to ask for my zero dollars back. [/ /] Also as a long-time series host I have 1,000 of these but I'm not drunk enough to share and might never be." Replying to @mocklerswriting. 8:34 a.m. 8 July 2019.

Singal, Jesse. @jessesingal. "Do you guys think it's good or bad to have a definition of 'violence' that includes both 'Kneeling on someone's neck until you murder them' and 'Releasing a statement about someone's murder that lacks a certain... je ne sais quoi'?" 8:390a.m. 12 June 2020.

Acknowledgments

Thank you to Shane Neilson for bringing this book into being. Thank you to Jeremy Luke Hill for everything he does. Thanks to the journals, magazines, conferences, and blogs that gave space to earlier, fragmentary, or altered forms of some of these essays: The Association of Canadian College and University Teachers of English Conference 2017 and 2018, The Association for Canadian and Québec Literatures Conference 2018, *Canadian Literature, Canadian Notes and Queries*, The Conference of Chinese/American Poetry and Poetics 2019, *My (Small Press) Writing Day, The Negative Review*, and *The Temz Review*.

About the Author

Carl Watts is from Hamilton, Ontario. He holds a PhD in English from Queen's University, where he wrote a dissertation about evolving conceptions of nationalism and ethnicity in twentieth-century Canadian fiction written in English. He currently teaches literature at Huazhong University of Science and Technology, in mainland China. His articles, book reviews, and poems have appeared in various Canadian, American, and British journals. He has published two poetry chapbooks, *Reissue* (Frog Hollow, 2016) and *Originals* (Anstruther, 2020), as well as a short monograph, *Oblique Identity: Form and Whiteness in Recent Canadian Poetry* (Frog Hollow, 2019). His more recent research interests include poetry subcultures, poetry anthologies, travel writing, expat communities, and addiction.